The Political Language of
Film and the Avant-Garde

Studies in Cinema, No. 30

Diane M. Kirkpatrick, Series Editor

Professor, History of Art
The University of Michigan

Other Titles in This Series

The Political Language of Film and the Avant-Garde

WITHDRAWN

by
Dana B. Polan
Assistant Professor
Department of English
University of Pittsburgh

UMI RESEARCH PRESS
Ann Arbor, Michigan

Produced and distributed by
UMI Research Press
an imprint of
University Microfilms International
A Xerox Information Resources Company
Ann Arbor, Michigan 48106

Library of Congress Cataloging in Publication Data

Polan, Dana B., 1953-
   The political language of film and the avant-garde.

   (Studies in cinema ; no. 30)
   Revision of thesis (Ph.D.)—Stanford University,
1981.
   Bibliography: p.
   Includes index.
   1. Moving-pictures—Political aspects.   2. Eisenstein,
Sergei, 1898-1948.   3. Brecht, Bertolt, 1898-1958.
4. Moving-picture plays—History and criticism.
I. Title.   II. Series.

PN1995.9.P6P65   1985   791.43'01   84-24062
ISBN 0-8357-1604-X (alk. paper)

For My Father and the Memory of My Mother

Contents

Acknowledgments

Parts of this study have appeared in different form in *Jump Cut, Cinema Journal,* and *Film Criticism.* My thanks to the editors of these journals for permission to now print reworked versions of those sections, and for their original interest in the work and for their helpful and perceptive feedback.

I am especially grateful to Professors Jean Franco, William M. Todd III, and Henry Breitrose, who throughout the process of this work were always instructive, perceptive, and receptive. The students in the Program in Modern Thought and Literature at Stanford University also deserve a special thank you. Michael Reuben, Michael Levenson, and Ron Imhoff, in particular, composed an excellent audience; each gave me essential suggestions.

To my wonderful colleagues Lucy Fischer, Paul Bové, and Marcia Landy, my gratitude.

Four scholars of film have especially sustained and contributed to my interest in film: Tania Modleski, David Rodowick, Ed Lowry, and Lea Jacobs.

My greatest "thank you" goes to Donie Durieu, for whom these words seem the most inadequate of signifiers.

1

Foundations

> ...the beginner who has learnt a new language always translates it back
> into his mother tongue, but he has assimilated the spirit of the new
> language and can produce freely in it only when he moves in it without
> remembering the old and forgets in it his ancestral tongue.
>
> Karl Marx, "The Eighteenth Brumaire of Louis Bonaparte"

Trying to create a new form of cinema, Sergei Eisenstein backs himself into a
corner; writing to his friend, Leon Moussinac, he tries to describe this new,
imagined cinema, and finds it virtually unspeakable: "this [new]
cinematography will be genetically ideological for its substance will be the
screening of.... Here's a kind of coup-de-théâtre: the one essential word in all
this hodgepodge doesn't come to mind ... okay, take the German word *Begriff*
(concept, idea)" (Eisenstein, quoted in Moussinac, p. 28).[1] Eisenstein's
dilemma is a common one. Eisenstein wants to move cinema away from
documentary realism or fictional escapism to the screening of something that
does not yet exist: an ideational cinema, a cinema which deals in
conceptualizations of the world.

The following pages work to suggest some of the ways to fill in the ellipses
of Eisenstein's call for a new form of cinema. I will discuss a number of
approaches which suggest that documentary realism, in its belief in a reality
that can communicate its own meanings, is politically limited; against the
empiricist faith that the reality of a situation can be revealed in the way it looks,
these approaches argue that a realism is only "really" achieved when what
seems actual is qualified, incorporated within a critical framework.

As soon as cinema theory and practice move beyond an understanding of
cinema as documentary reproduction and representation, the ideological
position(ing) of political cinema becomes ambiguous, difficult, problematic.
Unable to envision or accept the complexities of aesthetic mediation, a
tradition of sociologically oriented aesthetics kept art in the realm of the
representational. The formula is simple: to change consciousness, *show* a
political situation. (But what does it mean to *show* a situation? What aspect of
it? Is a situation showable?)

In Eisenstein's declaration we can find the attempt to give modern critical art a place—perhaps, as he tentatively suggests, to situate it at the level of the conceptual or ideational. Eisenstein's hesitation around a nondocumentary cinema which still wants to root itself in the social, is an emblematic one. It raises the question of the problematic conjuncture of materialism and modern art.[2] An essay in the etymological sense—an attempt, a foray—the following pages will try to find a place for a politicized aesthetic between an aesthetics of documentary reproduction (the world as show and as showable; the world as event to be "repeated" in art; the "real" as an attribute of the phenomenal) and the idealism of a post-structuralist freeplay (there is no "real" except in the play of signifiers, and in the position of the human subject for and in that play). Materialist aesthetics, I would suggest, is too often caught up in the epistemological problem of the "real"—how the "real" economic bases of the socius can or can't be captured within an artwork. But such an approach loses sight of the specificity of particular practices, such as aesthetic production— what Julia Kristeva (1976) calls "specific signifying practices." That is, it allows little place for understanding the material and political effectivity of forms, and too immediately collapses the formal onto the political. But, beyond that, the reduction of materialist analysis into a static epistemology (an unproblematic knowledge of objects of knowledge existing apart from the knower) ignores the (f)act of knowing as a practice in itself, as a material force which alters, in some sense makes, the very "things" it attempts to know; the place of the scientist is part of the meaning-process of the science. Against a definition of materialism (and materialist aesthetics) as an epistemology, as a knowing of *already constituted objects*, it is necessary to understand political practice as a *productive* activity that builds, more than it knows, its objects. Not really knowing about the true, materialism concerns itself with making and transforming a "true." This encounter with materialism as a science of production necessitates, then, a corresponding mutation in the objects of study: not really about objects, *things* at all, materialism is a practice which has practices as its object. Its field is the very way activities and the objects of activities structure meanings and relations.

In Marx's own writings, we find a practice (of writing) which deals with the material effect of social practices outside any reductive connection to material bases. In "The Eighteenth Brumaire," for example, Marx views people as faced with two very different relations to their living history (and to past history as a form which lives on in the present). What I will suggest is that these two ways are comparable to two political ways in which we can think of cinema theory and practice. On the one hand, Marx suggests that one way to live history is to do so in a kind of mechanical repetition, the present brought down by the past—history, Marx says, as a repetitive farce. This mode of being, of understanding, is a reproductive one. The present reiterates the past—indeed, owes its life to it—and therefore represents the past (and thus can itself be represented since it has an originary model—the "truth" of an earlier time— lying behind it). Like Freud's repetition compulsion, farcical history is a blockage in which the sins of the father, the originary tragedy, are passed on, as farce, to the children.

But against history as mechanistic repetition, another form of history is imaginable: history as a living of a moment in/through an active, transformative relation to the past, a relation of practice in which the materiality of historical existence is not merely cognized but changed (which is not yet to say anything about the ways it is changed). While a static history can be written about (the writing—the seizing upon an event as an already finished *thing*—being itself part of the continuation and transmission of the event), history as a practice in process is not really writable. Or, rather, one can write history—writing itself as practice, as a social act—but one cannot write *about* it. To write about history would imply its finality, its closure, its reification into thingness. Marx's own historical texts (for example, "The Eighteenth Brumaire," or "The Civil War in France") indeed are less reflections of a time than attempts at an intervention in it (writing as a race to keep up with history: Marx was able to present "The Civil War in France" as a lecture two days after the Commune had fallen.)

In such an approach, the object of science—the past, for example— becomes little more than the content of a convenient fiction in a very precise sense: as an explanatory model whose value lies not in its empirical verifiability but in its present and future usefulness.[3] As such, reproductions are amenable to rhetorical analysis: for example, Marx's own classification in "The Eighteenth Brumaire" of historical events according to genre (tragedy, farce). The past can be the province of aesthetics, of the study of closed symbolic actions. But as I've suggested, lived history is not writable, is not even susceptible to poetic analysis, is finally not in a relation of existence prior to or other than disciplines that would wish to constitute it. In such a framework, materialism takes its place not as a posterior science but as a part of the practice of history in process.

This conception, then, changes the role of the historian, the "critic" of society, from observer to participant.[4]

> Instead of asking: what is the position of a work *vis-à-vis* the productive relations of its time, does it underwrite these relations, is it reactionary or does it aspire to overthrow them, is it revolutionary?—instead of asking this question, or at any rate before this question, I should like to propose a different one. Before I ask: what is a work's position *vis-à-vis* the productive relations of its time, I should like to ask: what is its position within them? (Walter Benjamin, "The Author as Producer," 1977, p. 87)

With Marx and with Benjamin, we encounter a shift in the thinking of science from reproduction (in both the sense of maintenance and of imitation) of an a priori history to that of science itself as an activity in history, one which necessarily involves the power to change the field it operates upon. In this sense of science as a transforming activity, criticism and the aesthetic object will come together in the following pages. The theorists and practitioners of the cinema with whom I will deal often see cinema as a kind of science, indeed as a form which doesn't need posterior criticism since it is criticism itself. Eisenstein's call for a cinema of the *Begriff* is a call for a cinema which disdains intuition and the appreciation of phenomenal form to move instead toward a notion of the cinema as a language which can discourse about the social world as well as any other language system can. In the figures this study deals with, criticism and art necessarily blur; art here is no longer some mysterious other, some inhabitant of the realm of the inexplicit, of the overhead (as John Stuart Mill would have it). Criticism and art, I would suggest, are both fictions in Kermode's sense of fiction as an explanatory paradigm which shapes the phenomenal into some pattern. Yet, for all their fictiveness, criticism and art are no less subject to a criterion of social effectivity; fictive or not, paradigms come into the world with a force, a claim to authority, that needs to be evaluated. This is the point of Benjamin's declaration: it is less important to examine the epistemological verifiablity of a critical or aesthetic fiction than it is to examine the fiction's force, its power as an act (a power which may include, but is not necessarily limited to its epistemological content).

Where most post-structuralist theories of textuality see the productivity of the text as a bound-less process—Saussure's play of difference without positive terms—materialism's productivity, I would argue, is a building of new productive relations on the basis of the application and transformation of existing understanding. This last clause is an important one: the move from cognition (the province of epistemology) to practice (here the province of materialism as a science-in-process) is not a jump in which the old is rejected, left behind, but a transition in which original knowledge is mediated by a new way of seeing and, hopefully, a new way of acting. It is in this dialectical transition, which starts from and overcomes a given, that materialism, in one important way, distinguishes itself from the theory of textuality in post-structuralism (productivity as the generation of signifiers outside a social logic). While advanced materialism and post-structuralism share an emphasis on the new—new social relations, new discursive relations—it is also important to register the differences: this is especially true given post-structuralism's tendency to valorize a diversity of textual practices simply because they (seem to) reject rationalized and traditional codes of communication. (See, for example, Julia Kristeva's conflation of the discourse of the mad—*folle vérité*—the presymbolic babble of children, and the noncommunicative stance of modern poetry, all into the category of the semiotic or the polylogic.) This is the approach, as we shall see, by which an artist like Brecht, who argued for an art which would insert an internal gap *into* bourgeois art, and who called himself a realist, comes to be seen as a formalist theorist, his theory emptied of all its emphasis on social representation and its transformations by new theatrical practices.

When a theory of aesthetic productivity rejects documentary reproduction, it is not rejecting knowledge, but a confirming, static kind of knowledge (we see what we already know; our learning is redundant). A knowledge of a past, of prior history, can have its place in the production of the future, if it is knowledge of a past never before known (or known only in a wrong fashion). Thus, for example, Michel Foucault suggests that workers' documentary film is an important kind of cinema since it brings to light a cinema and a knowledge (in the content of the films) which was excluded by the rules of dominant discourses (see Foucault, "Interview on Film and Popular Memory," in Johnston, 1977). For Marx, the cure of history is to bring out that which has been unknown, not-known. It is a knowledge of the past that is not redundant, since, for the subject-of/participant-in history, it was never known in the first place; its only existence is in present knowledge retrospectively projected onto a past. Thus, what becomes important in regard to such a knowledge is not so much its epistemological relationship to a political past but its usefulness in the present; all history of the past is selection of the past. Materialism, in other words, can incorporate epistemology without becoming a posterior science; what materialism knows is not immediately given to it but is to be produced out of the immediately given. For Brecht, for example, modern theater is not a rejection of older social and representational codes for purposes of creating a totally new place for theater, but a playing-off of old representations against a qualification of those representations ("To speak as if one was making *quotations* of truth; that's what Father Brecht said"— Juliette in Godard's *Two or Three Things I Know About Her*, 1966.)

In such practice, then, cognition has its fundamental place as a ground, a base, for the play of the transforming, critical text against it; in Brechtian aesthetics, for example, the alienation-effect *requires* an initial situation which is (to be) alienated. This play between two orders of knowledge, the old and the new, is what allows the kind of Marxism Brecht espouses to be a nondocumentary realism; nondocumentary in its rejection of uncritical repetition; realist in its *incorporation* of the reproductive—which now becomes a content—into a larger critical framework which distances the reproductive from itself. In a shift which I will examine more closely in my discussion of Brecht (chapter 4), this kind of realism defines itself not immediately as a relation of social processes to a text which would represent them, but as a relation of one social text (ideology; a society's representations of itself; its mythologies) to another text which quotes the first and, so, alters it. By this detour of text against text, the Brechtian aesthetic hopes to create an art that struggles on its own terrain—the aesthetic—and not on another—that of economic relations in all their supposed transparency.[5]

All of this has consequences for the practice of film theory and criticism. If we define theory as Dudley Andrew does in *The Major Film Theories* (Andrew, 1976), as the means by which we make generalizations about the object of theory based on induction from some of its cases, then film theory can have little object; theories have no fixed object which they can know in a final, complete way. While, as material, there is certainly an *object* of film—namely, the film itself, the physical fact of celluloid which runs through a projector (a materiality which allows us to classify certain practices as films and others as something else)— the practice of film is no object, no thing, but a process, a positioning of text by spectator, and spectator by text. Most theories of film fail in their attempt to derive a general quality of film from what is usually no more than one aesthetic of one type of film (for example, Bazin's realist film).[6] The fiction film, for example, is actually not an entity but a particular kind of practice in which spectators shape mere shadows into usable fictions and constructs. At the same time that spectators constitute this object, work to engender this film, the film engenders them. Identity is identity-in-process; by producing its other (within the dual constraints of a social limitation on the nature and scope of production; and the partial independence of the object from the productive practices constituting it), the human subject produces itself. To continue with the example of the fiction film experience, by enabling—producing—the coherence of a film (for example, by reading it as story rather than the blur of textures and forms that it most immediately is), the spectator constructs him/herself as a spectator in pleasure, as someone enjoying the film. In such a process, both film and spectator are constituting contributors. (Later I will argue that formalism, a dominant mode of film theory, is precisely a move to sever the two aspects of this process, and to attribute all meaning-making value to qualities in films.)

The cinema is a set of specific signifying practices. Specific: that is, cinema and not some other practice. It is composed of a particular material; moreover, that material base provides certain means—what Metz calls *specific* codes—by which that material may be put into practice.[7] Signifying: that is, cinema shares with other practices the quality of being discursive. It is composed of signs which have as their main function to *address* the subject. Practices: the fact of film as a work, a production between film and spectator.[8] As a variable set of specific signifying practices, cinema cannot be confined to a theory, is not knowable; it is, as Raymond Bellour suggests, an unattainable text.[9] Paul Abbott describes some of the complexity of this process, this dialectic of text and spectator, and what it implies for film theory:

> What calls for theorization is the specificity of the historical localization, and this in turn demands analysis of the articulation of psychic elements...onto the practices and

calculations, and institutional forms which constitute the political system at issue. In question, then, is the engagement of the psyche in ideology, and the conditioning overlay of psyche, discourse, and political practice. . . . (Abbott, "Authority," *Screen*, 1979, p. 20)

But practice is always in excess of any hermeneutic which would attempt to know it. Thus, even a declaration like Abbott's reveals itself to be problematic in a certain incommensurability of two directions it sets up for film theory. On the one hand Abbott calls hopefully for the theorization of the "specificity of the historical localization." This is an idealist impossibility—the belief, the myth, that a moment can be known, fixed for the knower, objectified. Far more radical, and, to my mind, far more accurate, is Abbott's subsequent phrasing of historical complexity: "*in question* then is the engagement of the psyche in ideology. . . " (my emphasis). Knowledge is in question, that is, open(ed) to questioning.

Any activity will inevitably have to structure its object, to in some way decide that some aspects of its object are pertinent, more "objective," than others. But this search for what linguists call "pertinent units," significant divisions *in* the object of knowledge, is actually an interplay between the objecthood of the object known, *and* the objecthood of the knowing theory. The objecthood of the object is what I referred to earlier as the second of two constraints on the freedom of the act of production; against any subjectivizing understanding of the knowing subject's interaction with his/her world, materialism understands the objects of consciousness and activity as having an existence apart from, and prior to, a theory's interaction with them. There is always a margin in which the effects of one's actions—for example, interpretative activity—escape one's intentions because of the material intransigence of the material acted upon. In the practice of fiction, this material objectivity of the object shows up, to a large extent, as the "rhetoric of fiction," the force of fictional codes to construct and place the spectator or reader—what John Ellis calls "proffered codes" ("Made in Ealing," *Screen*, 1975). In part, this restriction of the "free" activity of the reader as producer relates to what I mentioned as the other constraint in productivity: "a social limitation on the nature and scope of production." The objective world into which any subject's praxis inserts itself is virtually a social world—the objects, the others, of one's experiences are always turning against one as an alienation shaped through the force of the *essential* otherness of experience. Indeed, self-identity, one's own self-defining, is immediately confronted by the limitations, the materiality, of one's insertion into a social situation, a class. In this sense, the self, like consciousness, is always already alienated from itself and bound to preexisting social definitions. For example, even hunger, a category seemingly bound only by biological necessity and the freedom of the hungry subject, is, as V.N. Voloshinov suggests in *Marxism and the Philosophy of Language*, alienated from the subject's personal freedom by the social ways he/she is able to experience hunger and to satisfy or not satisfy it (Voloshinov, 1973). Similarly, literary or film criticism is an activity in which the critic's situation determines the freedom of criticism. (For example, on a very broad level, the ability to be a critic, to spend one's time in that function, depends on a certain social privilege and social situation.)

On the other hand, any act, such as a theoretical act, is also a transforming force which escapes the impositions of rhetoric. A subject's activities escape the intentions, the impositions of a system. (But in what way? That is the question of practice, of the politics of intervention.) In part, this is so because any subject occupies several different social positions and functions. Also, as Hans Enzensberger suggests, a social system is no conspiratorial monster of intentionality which can contain the freedom of its members;[10] because dominant ideological practices only "proffer" codes, and don't try to achieve a complete ideological positioning of subjects, there is a kind of leakage, a subjectivity in excess of proffered subject positions.[11]

Even in knowing its objects, theory exceeds them. That this excess has a political ambiguity (what kind of excess; excess to what end?) explains in part why theory often expresses itself as an objective knowledge of its objects, and presents itself as knowing some*thing* in/about the objects of study. Faced with the complexities of signifying practices, with the ultimate indeterminacy of practice, theories will often divide out from the text a part which theory will then deem objective and objectively knowable, and another part which will be rejected as noise or valorized perhaps as an avant-garde subversion of the communicative aspects of the text. This attempt to make the indeterminate determinate, to find some*thing* in the text which theory can know (and evaluate) has, as we shall see, consequences for the way theories have understood the politics of aesthetic production and, subsequently, for the way they draw implications for future directions in aesthetic production.

Indeed, much of what passes in contemporary criticism as a critique of essentialism, of the positing of essential identities in a text, falls back into a sort of negative essentialism; upholding play, plurality, "le jeu infini du signifiant" (as Barthes puts it on the back cover of *S/Z*, 1971), such theory will posit this play as play *against*: against the objective presence of narrative, of representation, of illusionism, as givens of the text. That is, such theory sets up a number of objective characteristics of the so-called realist text (or narrative-representational-industrial text, as Claudine Eizykman calls it in *La Jouissance-cinéma*, 1976) against which the play of signifiers is said to be an opening up, a de-objectifying, a move from work to text as Barthes suggests ("From Work to Text," *Image/Music/Text*, 1977). But beyond its discovery of the plural text, an approach like Barthes's can engage in little critical qualification of the text, for such qualification would be a lessening of plurality. "About writerly [i.e., plural] texts, there is nothing to say perhaps. . . . The writerly text is not a thing. . . . It abolishes any criticism which, produced, would mix with it . . . " (*S/Z*, p. 11). However, almost as if to provide itself with a necessity, and therefore a justification, the theory of textuality always suggests that textual openness is achieved at a great cost: an escape from a less plural, less textual, more classical model. It is this model (what new film theory refers to when it talks of "the Hollywood paradigm") that can be analyzed, according to textual theory. Indeed, most of the structuralist and post-structuralist analyses have dealt not with the avant-garde text but with that ostensibly more coded, more rationalized art which the avant-garde is seen to be in reaction against; this is the context of such analyses as *Cahiers du Cinéma* on *Young Mr. Lincoln* or Raymond Bellour on *North by Northwest* (in *Communications* 23) or Stephen Heath on *Touch of Evil* ("Film and System: Terms of Analysis," *Screen*, 1975). In *S/Z*, we can see the process by which theory-as-knowing, as hermeneutic, infiltrates a more radical position of theory-as-part-of-textuality. From "Against Connotation," a section that assails any attempt to hold plurality within a limiting order, and rightly suggests that denotation is only another form of connotation, *S/Z* shifts into "For connotation, anyway," where order, as a hierarchial quality in/of the particular text, reemerges to provide a heuristic device by which the critic can control, can *know*, the various pluralities of texts. This dichotomy, the *scriptible* (writerly) against the *lisible* (readerly), shows up again in Barthes's codes: while the symbolic and semic codes have a pluralizing, dispersive effect on the text, the proiaretic and hermeneutic codes (and, to a lesser extent, the gnomic code) become objective structures of containment and closure.[12] While, as I have argued, divisions in a text are an inevitable consequence of the act of theorizing, and while all texts (as social texts and as acts of rhetoric) work to contain or close the work of the reader or spectator, the text's work is never objectively *in* particular figures or structures *in* the text. Stephen Heath and Gillian Skirrow's declaration that "there is a *generality* of ideology in the institution, 'before' the production of a particular ideological position" (Heath and Skirrow, "Television: A World in Action," *Screen*, 1977, p. 57) is a myth of formalism which gives texts a power that they only finally and really have in particular acts of being read.

Formalism is an empiricism in search of a justifying theory. Enumerating, describing materials, formalism assumes that meanings, consequences, implications, of textual practices derive foremost from those materials themselves; all that is required of the human participant—the spectator, the observer, the theorist—is the pertinent point of view, the framework appropriate to the object. In other words, a given form—for example, the invisible cut—has in formalist understanding a meaning in general, a meaning which, as in all empiricisms, is a logical consequence of the nature of the empirical object itself: to know the nature of a cut is to know its meaning. While critics like Barthes and Kristeva inflect this formalism by an attention to plural reading, to those ostensible moments in which the text escapes the impositions of set form, this kind of productive reading is no more than a modification in which the original formalism—generalities about the effects of narrative, about patterns of enunciation, about the tie between ideology and material objects—continues to hold sway.

A continual battle slogan in the practice of contemporary theory has been that it is concerned "not with what a text means, but how it means." I am suggesting that this change frequently does not confront the problem—that of the text as source, as origin, of meaning—but merely shifts attention from contents to structures, still seen *as attributes of a text itself.* Certainly, much of what in traditional film criticism passes for the study of meaning is little more than a kind of impoverished content analysis in which the presence of certain themes, subjects, values, is taken as a guarantee of the film's meaning; but the critique of content-analysis often redefines form as *really* being the content of a work and so proceeds within the same myth of objectivity. In his book, *Le filmique et le comique,* for example, Jean-Paul Simon has convincingly demonstrated the actual arbitrariness of content analysis. Citing and criticizing critics who declare that the Marx Brothers films are inherently revolutionary because of the presence of anarcic themes and subjects, Simon suggests that

> this bow to empiricism is never anything more than an avatar of an ideology of transparence (of social relations, or here of the signifier).... The cited analyses emphasize the critical and/or destructive aspects of the Marx Brothers without posing the question of the nature or support of this critique.... The universal comparison of an element in a film (or the ensemble of elements) to an element of the social structure is not enough to explain their relations or interactions. (Simon, 1979, p. 13)

Simon's solution is to try merely to make the *same* approach more rigorous by attention to "the film itself."[13]

Significantly, we can read in Simon's claim to return to "the film itself" the continued intrusion of another kind of analysis, a sort of return of the repressed (context). This return expresses itself as a recognition of the need to study "the *problem* of the relations which occur in the text *between* the productive instance, the produced instance, and the one it is produced for: the spectator" (p. 18, my emphasis). This conflict between two attitudes toward interpretation appears explicitly in Simon's next sentence where an initial recognition of the openness of the text, of its practice of meaning in real spectator contexts, is then repressed by a final recourse to formalism: "it's this circulation of the places of the producer [not the individual filmmaker so much as the whole enunciating apparatus of the text] and the receiver, marked in a filmic text, which we have tried to reconstruct, to recreate, by an attempt to construct *the formal apparatus* of cinematic enunciation" (p. 18, my emphasis). After his recognition that spectators and films create their meanings together, Simon then goes on to suggest that research on the formal attributes of films by themselves can lead to an understanding of meaning.

Formalism tends to have a peremptory effect on the understanding of film as a set of practices across a number of codes, both specific and nonspecific. If this were merely a shift of emphasis, an attention to an aspect of aesthetic production that previous criticism had ignored, then a temporary formalism might find its place in political criticism as a reminder of the material and political force of formal devices; for materialism, everything is political, and the study of devices as part of the political meaning of a work might serve as a useful corrective to an earlier, more content-oriented analysis that could only deal with those aspects of an artwork which seem nonspecific. In a critique of the work of Claire Johnston—work which emphasizes the presence or absence of subversive representations of women in film—Janet Bergstrom pinpoints the need for a shift to the operations of the text as a practice that is more than just a question of moments: "...narrative moments only take on their meanings from their value relative to the rest of the narrative.... It is a much simpler, and falsifying, model of meaning in film which takes interpreted narrative elements for 'narrative signifiers' than models closer to Freud's which recognize the kinds of processes which overdetermine, as well as repress, significance" (Janet Bergstrom, "Rereading the work of Claire Johnston," *Camera Obscura*, 1979a, p. 27).

The extreme of such formalism—the complete sundering of the open-ended and multiple indeterminate practice of film from certain codes granted objective status in the text—occurs in the work of Noel Burch, and in its explicitness we can read the limitations of formalist positions.[14] There's a moment for me in the work of Burch where the contradictions of his position—originally a descriptive one which made few explicit political claims for formal innovation, now a position which conflates formal innovation and revolutionary practice—emerge in all their obvious inadequacy. In *A Theory of Film Practice*, Burch describes television as solely a formal activity, a system of technical codes which interact among themselves and whose only real contact outside the formal structure of the particular work would be the previous formal tradition of those codes, the way codes operated in other works:[15] "By breaking down the barrier between genres and in particular by quite naturally introducing a mixture of the 'lived' and the 'staged,' television has encouraged the creation of new forms and structures based on a deliberate mixing of genres and materials in them and has begun to explore the multiple dialectics that can result from such a mixture" (Burch, 1971, p. 59). A social understanding of television, its place and insertion in the productive relations of a society (for example, the differing functions of television in the First and Third Worlds), disappears as a formalist understanding—history as the subversion in a closed space of aesthetic devices by new aesthetic devices—comes to dominate analysis. But what the practice of television "is" is not just a consequence of its forms and structures—just as hunger, as Voloshinov suggests, has no real meaning as an abstract category. Burch's newer book, *To the Distant Observer: Form and Meaning in the Japanese Cinema* (1979), pushes the separations further: Japanese films, with a rabidly militaristic and propagandistic subject matter, turn out to be fundamentally progressive and subversive in the way they play with forms (articulations of off-screen space; emphasis on non-narrative elements; rejection of depth in the image). This contradiction between two ways of understanding film reemerges as the potential incompatibility of the two goals of Burch's work. On the one hand, Burch echoes Roland Barthes's use in *L'Empire des signes* of Japan as a fictional construct: Burch approvingly quotes Barthes's declaration that one can "without claiming to represent or analyze any reality whatsoever . . . gather somewhere out in the world (. . .) a number of features (. . .) and with these features form a system. It is this system which I [Barthes] will call Japan." If, as I've suggested, any attempt to *know* a system "somewhere out in the world" is consigned to a certain fictiveness, a necessary incompleteness, then Burch's borrowing of an East as a system of codes useful for intervention in the practices of the West has nothing necessarily or inherently wrong with it. [16] But two hesitations must be raised. First, given that there is a living Japan, there may be a kind of cultural imperialism in Burch's attempt to construct a fictive Japan. Although as his title suggests, Burch tries to assume the position of a distant observer, this position of nonparticipant is constantly belied by his attempt to speak for the Japanese, to explain what their texts mean. [17] Thus, Burch declares that Japanese thought is lacking in theoretical insight or rigour—he talks of "the Japanese disdain of theoretical practice" (p. 12), and so he steps in to provide that theory: "One of the principal assumptions of this study is that the critical framework developed in France over the past decade (. . .) provides elements toward an understanding of the far-reaching theoretical implications of *le text japonais*" (p. 13). [18] Moreover, even if Burch's text reveals an inevitable fictiveness, it is necessary to evaluate the uses of that fiction; all theoretical work is fictive to an extent, but it has no less an effect in the particular modes of its insertion into the social. If all theory is selection, reduction, structuring, we can nonetheless ask the value of what has been selected, how it has been reduced, what has been structured. I've already suggested how this need to make distinctions, to search for objective pertinent units, shows up in much contemporary criticism as the setting up of a distinction between objective and closed structures in the work, and the valorization of a number of practices as subversive of that objectivity and closure. In Burch, this occurs as the objectification of narrative and illusionism as the defining characteristic of Western cinema: "The stages of formation and the on-going elaboration of the basic system [note the singular] of representation in the cinema of the West point to an all but universal tendency within the dominant cinema (as well as theatre and literature) to *maximize* and *generalize* the diegetic effect" (p. 19); "In the West, since the eighteenth century, our major narrative arts—the novel, the theatre, and more recently, the cinema have tended toward a kind of narrative saturation; every element is aimed at conveying, at expressing, a narrative essence" (p. 98). Against this, Burch will then single out as progressive elements in Japanese films which reject this "narrative saturation." Since, for him, it is this narrative saturation in and by a *form* which determines the political place of film, Burch can valorize otherwise reactionary films because they are formally innovative.

This attempt to read form against subject matter enters into direct contradiction with Burch's other goal: to write a real, objectively true *history* of Japanese cinema. ("My approach is, of course, historical in every sense," he says on p. 11, the first page of text.) But history, in most senses, cannot be written by a distant observer, especially when that distant observer (inevitably perhaps) structures the object of his/her history through (necessarily) different cultural structures; Burch reads his formal innovation/narrative closure split into the whole value system of Japanese culture without examining how or if this distinction might be relevant in another system. In this, it seems to me that he ignores a fundamental point about art's integration into a society's systems of representation, a point most clearly elucidated by Gombrich in *Art and Illusion*: namely, that what is considered to fit or "subvert" a society's representations is not something objectively defineable in the art itself, but rather is a definition by the society of the place of that art. Formal innovation is not some inherently progressive attribute of art at all places at all times; indeed, Gombrich's argument is that a particular way of seeing, as upheld by a culture, may lead to an overlooking of elements which don't fit the representational (realist or nonrealist) system. Whether one would want, with Gombrich, to call each society's particular way of seeing a "realism," one would, at the very least, have to recognize a conflict in the films Burch describes (or, more precisely, a conflict in the practice of the films) and study the actual parameters of reception in Japanese culture to understand how audiences actually resolve this conflict of form and subject matter.[19]

This criticism of Burch is not to suggest that formal analysis is irrelevant to political criticism. The deployment of specific codes in a film will be *a* source of the meaning-effect of the film, but only in their integration with other, nonspecific codes. For example, in *Cheyenne Autumn* (John Ford, 1964), a film which the filmmakers tried consciously to present a positive description of Indians, we can read the actual displacement of this project in the film's recourse to set figures of a certain kind of film exposition. The film, though about Indians, gives the voice of knowledge, the source of power and authority, to the whites. The opening shot of the film, for example, shows Indians walking while Richard Widmark's voice tells us why they are walking. Throughout the film, the Indian tale—not really cinematic by Hollywood standards—is displaced by a standard form—the love story of two whites. (This is not to imply that the love story form is inherently reactionary, but that often such a form, overdetermined by our society's uses of love, emerges to redirect other aspects of a story.) The last two shots of the film confirm this displacement, this unconscious ideology which can be read in the film: a shot shows the Widmark-Carroll Baker couple finally united in their love, with a young Indian girl (a symbol of the ostensible stake of the film) between them; in a cut to a closer shot, however, the Indian girl disappears out of frame, removed by the real stake of the story (the love of two whites separated by inconvenience). This is not to say that *Cheyenne Autumn* is definitely regressive *or* that it is definitely progressive; it is a reading of the film (here, my reading), facilitated but in no way determined or guaranteed by the presence of two different ideological practices, which makes the text. The point is that such an ideological practice of the text for a reader is neither a practice of form alone or of subject matter alone but of their particular articulation, an articulation never given to the text in advance of its being read. A narrative voice is not inherently a voice of authority,[20] and a cut of exclusion is not inherently a positive or negative act. In a lapse into formalism, Christian Metz suggests that offscreen characters invite audience identification since the audience is in a similar offscreen state (*Discourse*, "Interview with Christian Metz"), but this is to ignore the ways particular kinds of offscreen characters—for example, the monster lurking offscreen as the target of a frightened, onscreen character's look—might deflect any generalizable quality, if indeed such a generality exists, of identification.

In fact, a critique of formalism needs to render inadequate an implicit distinction in much current theory between form and content. Using the codes of narrative and realism, a film like *Z* (Costa-Gavras, 1969) will be said to be recuperated within a reactionary tradition, while a film like Godard's *Ici et Ailleurs* (1976), which is self-reflexively "about" the ways it can be about the P.L.O., will be said to be progressive at a more advanced level.[21] But no human practice is a collection of formal codes on the one hand and contents on the other; any particular practice, any textual system, is a combination and mutual displacement of elements into a new semiotic arrangement whose elements cannot be extracted except in an artificial and distorting way. A wave good-bye in a film derives its meaning not only from the social connotations of waving but also from the place of waving in the semiotic practice in the specific text of the film.[22] *Z*, for example, is not a film with the same old cinematic forms presenting a new content to the necessarily same old end or effect, but a unique text in which the meaning of elements exists in terms of their place in the text where it is impossible to isolate elements as content or form. To take a more immediate example, while a television show like *All in the Family* used, and repeated, many of the available specific codes of television storytelling (for example, consistent screen direction; definable beginnings, middles, and ends) and so could be said to adhere to an old system of representation, the very introduction of new elements—even if they are elements nonspecific to television (for example, the image of the bigot, the working class accent)—changes that old system; the presence of a new accent on television, for example, becomes part of the textual system, gives the show part of its meaning in a way that is not distinguishable as content or as form.[23] This, however, is not to claim that this new textual system, simply by being new, is in any way inherently subversive of the old. Every message, by not being some other message, is again a *differance*, a meaning which defers (is like the preexisting) but differs (is unlike the preexisting); the effect of any particular semiotic arrangement is never given in advance to a text by its adherence (or not) to prior codes, but can only exist in relation to the specific interaction of that text's codical arrangement with other codes (specific and nonspecific) *and* in the relation of the specific textual system to the whole social semiotics of an historical moment.

The example of Noel Burch's formalism, although extreme, stands as an indication of the political consequences of the adoption of any formalist position, any position which attempts to prescribe objective meanings to set structures in the practice of the text. Theories of film serve as justifications of particular aesthetics, particular norms, calls for particular kinds of filmmaking. I will have occasion to return to some of the implications throughout the course of this study.[24] In the chapter on Brecht, for example, I will suggest that a certain objectification of pleasure as a reactionary form has led, with a misuse of Brecht, to the encouraging of cinematic practices which explicitly attack pleasure and its relations to action. The point is not to valorize pleasure as an unproblematic category, but precisely the opposite, to suggest that no general theory—positive or negative—of pleasure, or any other category *as category*, should be the goal of film theory.

As already suggested, much of the attack on imputed objective structures is an attack against narrative, against what Frank Kermode will call end-determination—a kind of Hegelian finality which comes to make sense of, to contain, the textual energy of a particular textual practice. Stephen Heath, quoting Michael Snow's remark that events "take place," suggests that narrative is literally an act of taking places, of *appropriation*, in which the development of a story brings into (literal) view new sights which the film takes over and controls. Central to this premise is a reading of the kind of control of the new, the different, that ostensibly occurs in shot/reaction shot editing; in this reading, offscreen space, as unknown, unviewed, and therefore unavailable to the spectator's fetishistic look, is a threat, an excess, to the centering of vision in the narrative. The shot/reaction shot works to contain this threat; a character's look invokes the offscreen space only so that the film can show that space in the next shot as implicated in the logic of the story. For Heath, "the power of such an apparatus is in the play it both proposes and controls: a certain mobility is given but followed out—relayed—as the possibility of a constant hold on the spectator, as the bind of a coherence of vision, of, exactly, a vision" ("The Question Oshima," 1978, p. 76). But, again, this can essentialize specific codes, separate form and content, and limit film to only one kind of practice (a play within a more dominant closure).

Heath's argument for the power of the cinematic apparatus in its containment of mobility through vision rests on two potentially essentializing premises about such an apparatus of cinema. First, the premise that there is indeed such an apparatus, that a general model or "institution" of cinema exists; this is the supposition that there is a paradigmatic form, a norm—what current theory calls "the classical Hollywood model" or the "Hollywood paradigm." This paradigm, this ideal form, is considered as such because of its imputed normalization of systems of representation through narrative and realism. But what most close readings of films, including imputed Hollywood classics, can reveal is the ways in which films exceed, violate, rules imputed to the films from outside by theory; not so much a play *against* a classic model, excess is rather the very quality of films as acts. This is not to suggest that films do not fall into types—that, for example, a genre theory of film would be impossible. Rather, genre itself has to be seen as a site of difference, of play. The very way we constitute film genres in our everyday viewing experience is a recognition of the arbitrariness of any modelling; from one moment to the next, a film will be deemed a Western or a Cary Grant film or a comedy, as if these were compatible categories. The experience of genre is an interplay between generic norms (themselves always varying) and the ways individual texts escape, play with, these norms.

In a useful critique of the notion of *langue*, of the set of codes supposedly determining the communication act, Charles Altman has suggested that any reading of a text is not a reading according to *langue* but a *displacement* of *langue* by the particular parameters of a text (Altman, "Intratextual Rewriting: Textuality as Language Formation"). As Altman suggests, reading is a decoding of elements not only according to their set linguistic values; it is also a communication based on a commutation of the particular value of linguistic elements *in position* in the text. Thus, "intertextual" meaning, as Altman calls this production of meaning by a play of differences across the text itself, counters the domination of *langue*, the assignation of all meanings to mere actualizations or applications of general rules. This suggests the second essentialist aspect of Heath's approach: beyond objectifying certain techniques and structures as being the real identity of a certain cinema, Heath goes on to suggest that these supposedly invariant structures also have unvarying *effects*, that they always produce the same meanings. In other words, independent of its intratextual place, any element is supposed to work always to the same end. (For example, Metz's offscreen character always invites primary identification.) Narrative, for example, will always serve to take places, to control, to seize up difference.

Ultimately, I would suggest, a problem with Heath's position is that it is based, implicitly, on a particular philosophy and politics of subjectivity and consciousness which underlie the way he thinks out the specific interventions of film. Coming at the end of a long tradition which critiques individuality and the sovereignity of consciousness, the kind of film theory in which Heath and others engage defines the politically regressive primarily as that which upholds the unity of consciousness, the sanctity of the self, the wholeness of being, against loss, dispersion, dissemination, difference; in this perspective, the Western tradition, and its politics, is seen as an order of reason, of rationalism. Cinema is then one of the practices which works against dissolution of the subject, and is therefore one of the sites which is deemed to need subversion by a different practice of cinema, by a cinema of complex difference. My argument is that it is precisely in the original philosophical suppositions about the relations between politics and subjectivity that current theory has too quickly made assumptions about what is progressive and what is regressive; we can find in the underlying philosophy a practice of closure, not so much in the objects, as in the theory reflecting back onto the objects of theory. To assume that the imposition of reason is the sole (or even primary) way in which political power exercises control is again to essentialize, to idealize identity—this time in a most literal sense, since it is the originary assumption that *identity*, selfness, is the sole origin from which reactionary practice derives, which leads to all other assumptions (for example, the valorization of difference). Heath's argument is that a certain structure of cinema supports a certain space of politics. I am suggesting that this "theory" of film practice is challengeable, both in the way it understands the moments of this ostensible process and in the way it understands the relations—the supports—between moments. Even if we grant the existence of a Hollywood paradigm, this is not necessarily to say anything about the effects, the supports in viewer consciousness, of this paradigm. Indeed, in his *Procès du spectacle*, Christian Zimmer goes so far as to suggest that a coherence of film, a logic of apparatus, might work not so much to align the coherence of the spectator, but precisely to disturb it, to put the spectator in a position of incoherence, all the better to maintain social distinctions. More precisely, Zimmer suggests that the cinema, as a force of social positioning, presents unattainable images to its spectators specifically to produce a kind of loss, a sense of inferiority. For Zimmer, cinema is not escapism but, quite the contrary, a practice which devastatingly reminds the spectator of the impossibility of escape; it is a practice that works to put barriers between objects and possession of them by converting objects into mere images, simulacra, which audiences will return to in a virtually masochistic resignation.[25] This is not to argue that Zimmer is "essentially" right. In fact, his position may err too far in another conspiratorial direction, seeing the cinema as a plot to encourage inferiority and self-loss. Rather, it is simply to note that alternate readings of cinematic politics are possible, and that every definition of progress and regress will rely on some prior, more originary philosophy which needs to be examined and evaluated.

In a rejoinder to the argument that there is a political inevitability to film techniques, Philip Rosen has shown how one cut in *Seventh Heaven* (Frank Borzage, 1927), a seemingly classic film that received Oscar nominations in the first year of the Oscars, undermines the previous coherence of the film's narrative (Rosen, "Difference and Displacement in *Seventh Heaven*," *Screen*, 1977). *Seventh Heaven* deals with two lovers separated by war who deny any danger to their situation because their love is higher and stronger than all other forces, including religion. The hero is gravely wounded at the front, and a priest administers the last rites. In the next scene, the priest goes to the girlfriend back in the States to tell of the boyfriend's death, and, now on her own, the girlfriend begins to accept the courtship of another man. Cut to: the hero struggling through a crowd to get home, not really dead after all. Rosen reads this ultimate contradiction of material necessity as a consequence of Borzage's contradictory ideological beliefs as both a materialist and a spiritualist. Although perhaps a little too reliant on biographical information and authorial psychology, Rosen's reading of *contradiction* is nonetheless an important one because it emphasizes the contradictory insertion of any text into social practice, and the contradictory place of any particular technique in the intratext of the film. Intratextually, the cut here serves as a nodal point between two very different textual systems (and their respective systems of representation): it violates the continuity of one story (that of a material world and its necessities in which the dead stay dead) and reestablishes the continuity of another (a love story which knows no bounds, not even the bounds of probability and logic). In contrast to this open-ended understanding of the politics of technique, formalism tries to freeze politics, treating certain textual practices as essences, and so ends up as virtually a more theoretically refined version of manipulation theory: manipulating texts on one side, tied to an order of representation; manipulated spectators on the other side, tied to the text. But Rosen's point is that texts don't express or practice *an* ideology; they exist as part of ideological practices, a *plurality* of effects which differ for each different insertion of the text into social practices. Any text is internally contradictory because the social field is contradictory. As Michel Pecheux suggests, "ideological state apparati are not so many pure instruments of the dominant class, ideological machines purely and simply reproducing existing relations of production.... Ideological state apparati constitute— simultaneously and contradictorily—the ideological place and condition for the *transformation* of relations of production..." (*Les verités de la palice*, p. 129, my emphasis).

Formalism, however, can only recognize external contradiction; for formalism, the cinema is a given, an institution working to set ends, a fixed signifier which is coherent in its practice. Contradiction, in this formalism, is either something that the text generates, the better to hold it in place, or something that can only assail the institution of cinema from outside, from elsewhere, as negativity, as difference. What happens to the conception of progressive art in such a schema is revealing; coming upon a preexisting, monolithic form, oppositional art can only be understood in formalist theory as an excess, a surface disturbance of the monolith. For Julia Kristeva, for example, productivity is little more than a vertical dimension which impedes the more central, horizontal narrative progress of the text: "the 'text' (poetic, literary, or otherwise) hollows out in the surface of the word a vertical where is established those models of *significance* which communicative and representative language *cannot speak*" ("Le texte et sa science," 1969, p. 11). Here the communication act itself is posited as unproblematic, a simple and controlling flow of information from one fixed pole to another—a fixity which poetry *then* disturbs.

More than that, as a critique of rationality, this contemporary theory can give an exaggerated recognition to the very rationality it is setting out to critique. It assumes, in other words, that the ideological effect of a social practice, as either supportive or deconstructive of an *articulated* logic, lies in its relation to rationalism alone. Politics becomes a battle of the coded against that which escapes the coded; the existing political system becomes a place of homogeneity, coherence, organization, while subversion becomes the realm of the alogical, the transrational, the noneconomic.[26] This sets up a sharp dichotomy, an either/or which is problematic both as a dichotomy and in the values or qualities it assigns to respective terms. Is it true that the ideological practice of "Western society" (if such a unity even exists as contemporary theory contends) is a practice of rationality?[27] Such a perspective, as I've suggested, would seem to ignore the question of contradiction: social practices are not essences, expressions of a basic ideological meaning, but sites of struggle in which a single practice can function to very different ends. There are contradictions, for example, in a particular class society and its projects; to cite just one, historians have shown that capitalism is often torn between two goals—increased production and increased consumption—which then necessitates other practices to evolve to attempt to resolve the contradiction (in this case, advertising and media.)[28] Further, there are contradictions regarding the function of a practice for different classes; to use a case from aesthetic production, nineteenth-century realism can be read either as part of the capitalist's myth of political economy—that subjects are actually economically free individuals—*or* as the first literature, widely available, in which working classes can see themselves and their struggles discussed and, perhaps, confirmed.[29]

All practices can have progressive and regressive potential; this is to say, among other things, that no political system is coherently rational, and that, as important, irrationality is not inherently an oppositional force. Irrationality can be an unconscious excess intruding into particular ideological projects. For example, as I will clarify later, we can read in many films the presence of two texts: the manifest text with one logic, and a subtext, often a subversive text, with a different or counterlogic.[30] But irrationality can equally be a fundamental and necessary part of a social system, excess there serving as a kind of stopgap in which a system which is itself excessive can renovate itself. This, for example, is the argument that Jean-François Lyotard raises against Kristeva's valorization of the alogic of semiotic discourse.[31] For Lyotard, the social system is always both logical and alogical—a division constituted along the line of sexual difference, relegating women to the realm of the emotional, the nonproductive, and thus confirming a necessary social arrangement.

Roland Barthes, in his essay "The Third Meaning in Some Stills of Eisenstein," finds, *against* symbolic or narrative meanings, what he calls an obtuse meaning, "a kind of blunting of a too-obvious meaning. . . . The obtuse meaning is clearly counter-narrative itself" (Barthes, 1977, p. 63). As Kristin Thompson points out, this notion of obtuse meaning reiterates the Russian Formalist notion of delay, of aesthetic devices as an impediment to direct narrative progression (Thompson, "The Concept of Cinematic Excess, *Cine-Tracts*, 1977). But it is important to note that for the Formalists there was often a tendency to extend the qualities of *ostranenie* from particular works to the whole of the aesthetic dimension itself—that is, there was an implicit (Kantian-inspired) recognition that art tended toward the nonpurposive, that in this obtuseness lay not a specific, politically progressive strategy but a general founding quality of art as art. What for the Formalists was a basically apolitical investigation of conditions of art, however, becomes in contemporary theory a conflation of formalism and politics.

This is to suggest that bluntness, estrangement, impediment, irrationality, and any other qualities to which an anti-economic function in art is attributed are in fact potentially socially functional or supportive qualities. In some way, what has happened in the critique of film in contemporary theory is similar to what Jean Baudrillard sees as often happening in the Marxist critique of political economy; out of the multitude of practices that constitute the political space of a society, one practice which is easily codifiable (e.g., narrative as a defined succession of units; visual representation as an effect of the mathematically calculable parameters of perspective; political economy as based on analyzable patterns of production and exchange) is isolated from the complicated field of the interaction of practices and made to seem determinate, made to be the source and logic for all other practices.[32] Against this determinism and domination by one form said to be logical—said to be logic, origin, in itself—Baudrillard suggests that politics and political control is not so much a matter of logic but of fluidity, a free-floating exchange and production of signs, whose political meaning lies in the fact that they have no one meaning; that is, instead of situating values in one place, they situate them in contradiction, in many places at the same time. For Baudrillard, economy is only one localized process in a broader play of processes which may be as much in excess of economic determination as they are inside economics. And yet, this freeplay is nonetheless political, nonetheless "economic" on a wider scale; at the very least, Baudrillard suggests, fluidity has to be seen as a strategy in the game of social distinction where some groups actually possess power while other groups mimic this possession in the realm of signs, not realizing that their ability to manipulate signs, to generate new signs, to play, is no real power at all, but only its alibi.[33] Baudrillard's understanding of politics seems not so much a rejection of a base/superstructure model, as a *reversal* of that model, economics and value becoming only one aspect of a social base now understood as the whole realm of meaning and sign production, which includes aesthetic practice, the production of exchange value, the entire range of symbolic activity: "The quantification of vision, connected to its 'passivity,' refers back to a socio-economic imperative of usefulness, refers back to the *object-of-capital*, but this 'capitalization' may be nothing more than an overdetermination of a deeper social constraint, which is that of symbolic force, of social command, of *mana* which itself attaches to the *object-as-fetish*" (*Pour une critique*, p. 48). Where the model of determinism tries to collapse the difference of the superstructure onto the sameness of the base, Baudrillard's approach starts from the recognition of difference, of excess, as the initially political, as the social field in which particular strategies, always internally and externally contradictory, take form. Baudrillard achieves, then, an uneven reversal of the base/superstructure model, since the "base," if it can still be understood as such, is now a dispersive field, a place of logic *and* alogic, of rational *and* presymbolic (or semiotic in Kristeva's sense), of value *and* sign.

Marx expressed bewilderment at his own continued admiration for Greek art; this admiration, which didn't seem to fit the notion of art as a superstructure of a particular and therefore nontransferable structure of society, was for Marx a problem, and many Marxist aestheticians have felt it necessary to start from this problem in order to preserve the reflection model, perhaps by opening up the model through a recognition of "relative autonomy."[34] In this lengthening of the model—the interposition of "determination in the last instance"—a recognition of the excessive, of the way in which practices don't "fit," intrudes into the original Marxist model and alters its initially economic position.

Despite their differences, the Althusserian and Baudrillardian understandings of art are not ultimately irreconcilable.[35] Trying to explain why, if society is fundamentally economic in the base, a superstructure would have any function or place or origin at all, Althusser is led to the convenient fiction of "determination in the last instance." The superstructure serves as an interpolating, positioning force to assure the mental and physical disposition of workers for the necessary reproduction of the forces of production. But Althusser's argument is not so much an answer as a displacing of the question. At nodal points, the contradictions of this displacing, which stays with the context of the original problem, show forth. What happens to art in the Althusserian position is significant; where other forces of the superstructure (repressive and ideological state apparati) work toward the preservation of the base, art is somehow magically other, safe from a function of manipulation. Art becomes the realm furthest from determinism, furthest from a function *for* the base—a realm which, therefore, can somehow come to serve as a critique of that very base.[36] At its limit, Althusser's characterization of art approaches Baudrillard's in its recognition of the nonpurposiveness of art, in its rejection of value as use. Art is no longer necessarily a tool of the base:

> What art makes us see, and therefore gives us in the form of *'seeing,' "perceiving,'* and *'feeling'* (which is not the form of *knowing*) is the ideology from which it is born, in which it bathes, from which it detaches itself as art, and to which it alludes.... Balzac and Solzhenitsyn give us a 'view' of the ideology to which their work alludes and with which it is constantly fed, a view which presupposes a *retreat*, an *internal distantiation*, from the very ideology from which their novels emerged. (Althusser, "A Letter on Art..." (1971) pp. 222-23)

There is in the Althusserian position, I would suggest, a recognition—often repressed—of a different model for art than an economic one; the magic of art is one of the points of that recognition. As Baudrillard suggests, Althusser may be caught within a mirror of production—political economy and its theorization each mirroring and determining the economism, the logicism, of the other—but one which is a virtually secondary revision of a more fundamental, anti-economist mode of understanding.

To reiterate, Baudrillard does not so much remove attention to the political, as displace it: the political becomes *more* than an equivalent to the merely economic. What in his description of commodities might seem a reversion to a kind of Sontagian fascination with the erotics of surface or a Bachelardian mythology of ideal substances (for example, Baudrillard's virtually poetic evocation of such qualities as the *polished* and the *varnished*, or his attention to the saturation in daily life of covers—tablecloths, place-mats, bedsheets, etc) is actually the creation of a political *phenomenology*.[37] The phenomenological descriptions, the flights into a virtual poetry, are nothing but so many attempts to evolve a nonreductive, noneconomic language to describe aspects in the politics of commodities beyond their use-value, aspects other than their economic insertion:

> Objects enter into a perpetual game, which results in fact from a moral conflict, a disparity of social imperatives: the functional object pretends to be decorative, dresses itself up in

uselessness or travesties of usefulness—on the other hand, the futile and idle is charged with a practical reason ... in this paradoxical determination, objects are thus the place, not of the satisfaction of needs, but of a symbolic work, a "production."...(ibid., pp. 12-13)

What contemporary theory will valorize as play, as excess, Baudrillard therefore sees as a potentially reinforcing component of social position; the sliding of the signifier (Lacan), the shifting of signs, makes a nice fit with the way capitalism can impose values simply by a change of names, by a recourse to the new, the different. Bound to a real order of class, not trying to change social structure, people accept the compromise position of change at the level of signs, not realizing that a play with signs, an attempt to change values through signs, may be a detour; like Saussure's understanding of language as a play of negative terms with no effect on a positivity (the real beyond and behind the referent), Baudrillard's conception of symbolic exchange is that of an endless play, a continued substitution which cannot break out of infinite circulation in the realm of signs to engage in any kind of effective praxis; signification is potentially independent of the position of its players, and it is this separation that gives the effective structures of social distinction their endurance: "This false dynamic is in fact completely overrun by the inertia of an unchangeable social system and its discrimination in the realm of real power" (ibid., p. 55).

If we look at much contemporary theory from the perspective of sign exchange, we can see how this theory can duplicate the reification and separation of the economic out from the fluidity of the political. Indeed, the very focus on narrative as a central site in the containment of excess is a central component in the political economy of much contemporary film criticism. Not only metaphorically but literally, narrative becomes the economic center of film, its good story, its salability, its source of reaction. In his essay "Acinema" (1978), Jean-François Lyotard goes so far as to suggest that, as a succession of units, narrative is fundamentally an economic activity, tied to an order of exchange-value: each moment of the story is exchanged for the next, every moment has its function in the whole. Lyotard consequently valorizes the nonsuccessiveness of serially organized films, on the one hand, or structurally minimal films on the other. These, he argues, are cinematic forms which refuse exchange. Lyotard falls into the recurrent essentialism of such a position; all narrative is bad, all nonnarrative is good—a position which leads him to accept as progressive the Scandinavian practice of *posering*—nude women posing motionless for the look of men—simply because there is no motion, no narrative, in the activity.[38]

In his essay "En sortant du cinema," Roland Barthes argues that the central, repressive function of film is its holding of the spectator in place to an order of representation, a mirrorlike activity: "the image captivates me, captures me, I *adhere* to the representation, and it is this adherence which founds the *naturalism* (the pseudo-nature) of the filmed scene..." (Barthes, *Communications*, 1975, p. 106). Barthes is then able to suggest that a different attitude in the spectator, an attention to an other scene of the film experience, would cut against this: "I have two bodies at the same time: a narcissistic body which looks [regard], lost in the close mirror, and a perverse body, ready to fetishize not the image, but precisely that which exceeds it: the grain of sound, the auditorium, the blackness, the obscure mass of other bodies, the rays of light, the coming, the going . . . " (ibid). But this has always been part of the dominant filmgoing experience, one of the effects we go to movies for: that fascination of story *plus a something more*, from the posters outside to the type of theater (a factor leading in the twenties and thirties to the construction of "movie palaces"), to the inclusion of sensory orders other than seeing and hearing, in the form of taste (the food one eats) and touch (the softness of seats, for example). This phenomenological plenitude, this richness of experience, may exceed the logic of narrative but it is not, for all that, politically *excessive*. The whole act of going to films as a *Gesamtkunstwerk* can fall short of disturbing the social sense of moviegoing and is in fact its sense—movies as the moment when, beyond the logic of work, all logic gives way. While it is no doubt possible, as Umberto Eco suggests, to show how images are coded, structured, at a number of levels,[39] this approach ignores the possibility that the "meaning," if we can still call it that, of images lies in a richness of freeplay, in precisely their irreducibility to structures. The offer of a "good" film is the offer of a constant flux of signs in which logic, illogic, sight and sound mix together in a pell-mell fashion. There is something economic about this: we pay money to see films, and then judge whether or not they were worth a certain expenditure. But this economy is one of plenitude—we pay a little to get a lot (for example, in the case of a literary adaptation, we pay to get more than what was in the book). What Baudrillard says of other commodities can extend to the plurality of the film spectacle: "At a final level, aesthetic privilege is no longer attached to the varnished, nor to the rough, but to the liberty to freely combine all terms . . . all combinations are possible" (p. 35). In a film like Vincente Minnelli's *Yolanda and the Thief* (1945), the rigor of storyline becomes only one sign among many—the dances, the multiplications of characters, the movement of camera which constantly brings into sight new sights. What "takes place" in such a film is not narrative but that complex aesthetic activity in which all combinations seem possible; each shot, each movement, is not a narrativization of space but an accumulation of spaces into a flux which surpasses narrative alone. In this sense, the spectacle of film realizes one of the premises of the Russian Formalists: namely, that all elements in the film, elements of subject matter as well as elements of form, become aesthetic devices—the recourse to a certain kind of character psychology, for example, becomes virtually a peg to build a particular aesthetic object, an effect, a ground.

Films tend to be in excess of any of their codes, tend toward a surplus of signification. The aesthetic dimension, far from holding human subjects in place, positioning them, may well be an area which disperses the subject, engages in his/her *loss*. In this dispersion, the filmwork is both progressive and regressive: regressive in that it provides a false realm of freedom from representation by allowing one to think that change is merely a matter of change in and through signs; progressive in that it therefore stands as a reminder of the incompleteness, the limits of representation. As Pierre Macherey and Marcuse suggest in different ways, art can serve as an unhappy consciousness, measuring the nature of social loss.[40]

If the artwork can be called a sign system, then it is not only because the artwork is a text that sets up an order of signifiers bound to an order of signifieds (process of denotation and connotation), but because, beyond real positions (class, the force of the social), art is the site of an unbinding, signifiers and signifieds dispersed beyond signification into a (dis)order of affect, a play beyond system. Reading against the impressionism, the subjectivism, of earlier film criticism, contemporary film theory tried to establish itself as a science by recourse to structural analysis, to the study of codes and meaning-production.[41] But this structural emphasis occurs at the price of a reduction, a misconception of the original object of study (which is no coded object at all).

This is not at all to suggest that there isn't a logic (or logics) somewhere in the text of a film. Nor is it to suggest that the political practice of film lies solely in its spectacle, in its symbolic play of signs—in short, that the film offers no specific meanings, particular images, as part of its ideological practice. With an unquestionable insistence, image studies—for example, the various studies of the *image* of women in film, of positive or negative images—have demonstrated the social use of objects of vision as mythic objects (in Barthes's sense of the myth as the conversion of the natural into the cultural). In their analysis of *Yesterday's Children*, a British television show about truancy, Heath and Skirrow ("Television: A World in Action," 1977) cite a moment in the show (ostensibly a balanced, objective documentary) where politics seems to emerge in all its virtually propagandistic bluntness—a bluntness which could appear to put to rest all arguments about validity in interpretation, about multiplicities of meaning. A scene shows Linda, one of the truants the program is about, escaping to a boutique where she spends the afternoon trying on clothes. Heath and Skirrow note how this sequence, showing the only girl truant in the program, shows her differently from the boys: slick music comes on the soundtrack for the first time, and the montage speeds up, fragmenting Linda's body through closeups of her pelvis and breasts. For Heath and Skirrow, this moment is unambiguous: "an absolute moment of spectacle with special terms of attention, meaning, and enjoyment for the viewer" (p. 32).

Such a moment, in effect, seems unquestionably sexist; but is precisely *in effect* that it is so—in practice, in a specific act of being read, and not in any essential meaning of the image. This is why criticism (such as Heath's and Skirrow's) can at all take a distance from the proffered meaning, and read the scene *against* its original intention. The scene's sexism is never more than proffered, and Heath and Skirrow reject the offer to come up with a different reading. The meaning of an aesthetic moments is an interaction between the rhetoric of that moment, its place in the intratext, and its relation to the mythic intertext of a society and its hermeneutics. Intratextually, a scene's meaning depends not on its own qualities as scene alone but on its difference across the text. Indeed, the procedure of much demythicizing art is not to reject myths but to situate them differently, to alter their place within the intratext. For example, in *The Act of Seeing with One's Own Eyes* (1971), Stan Brakhage works specifically to alter the kind of attitude we normally hold regarding the human body as a site of beauty and inviolate integrity. Set in the Pittsburgh autopsy room, *Act of Seeing* shows the body as inert matter, as material to be acted upon by the tools of the coroner. That Brakhage intends the film as a transcendental experience, a creation for the spectator of vision freed of mediated ways of seeing (the title is a literal translation of the original Greek root of *autopsy*), may be less important perhaps than the effect of the film to challenge specific cultural attitudes toward the body. One scene, which could stand as a critique of the kind of visual pleasure in the female body offered to the spectator in *Yesterday's Children*, begins on a closeup of a woman's genital region, her legs spread apart; but any sexual resonance to this scene is very quickly thrown into disarray as the camera pans up the woman's midriff, which has been opened up by the coroner's knife. The place of a tauntingly erotic approach to the body is thereby challenged by another image of the body.

The mythic meaning of an image depends upon the existence of a supporting myth and possibilities for reading that myth in accordance with the general system of social values existing prior to the particular image. As Barthes explains it, myth is a particular connotational meaning of a signification; as signifier, any image can signify any number of signifieds, but myth will function to hold that signification into a particular order, to a held connotation.[42] There is a strangely disquieting moment in *Killer's Kiss* (Stanley Kubrick, 1955) where the kind of fetishizing of the body seen in *Yesterday's Children* does not work because there is no support in connotation for the particular signification at this moment: as the boxer-hero gets ready for a match, the camera moves in for a close-up of his torso and then lovingly moves up and down his body. The scene can be disturbing; it is a technique for the presentation of the body such as we have often seen in films, but this time it is an image of a man and not a woman. Without a connotational field to support it, the scene can call into question the seeming naturalness of the way women have been similarly represented in film.[43]

The intratextual and social contexts of meaning demonstrate that any meaning is relative, sustained not by an essence, but by a placement. Yet, this is still not to explain the fact that certain meanings can have a power inside the fundamentally dispersive field of art. In other words, if, as I've suggested, one of the political functions of art is to disperse signs, to offer a freeplay of signification, this function might seem to be in direct contradiction with the function of myth as the fixing of signs to a particular order of meaning. Indeed, in certain texts, one can see a conflict of myth and dispersion, the text trying to be both value and mere sign at one and the same time. In such cases, the conflict of political functions can emerge in all its potential contradictoriness; this, for example, is part of the interest of the films of Sam Fuller, where one senses an incompatibility between the story as B-movie entertainment and the pretensions in the films to serious messages upholding the American dream.[44] In *The Crimson Kimono* (1959), for example, a film that seems to be a complicated detective story set in Los Angeles's Chinatown, there are awkward intrusions by morality, when the baroqueness of camerawork and narrative voice suddenly settles down to reverently allow the message to speak unhampered. But the virtual arbitrariness of these moments, their disintegration inside an irreverent intratext, removes their force: the baroqueness infiltrates and alters the quiet moments, tinges them with a corrupt weirdness. Morality, and the need for films to be moral, is potentially brought into question.

Myth and dispersion can, however, be compatible aspects of a text's political practice. I have already suggested that dispersion can function as an activity of social distinction by offering a spectacle in which no distinctions hold, in which all meanings are upset. For example, in Gregory La Cava's *My Man Godfrey* (1936), boundaries between rich and poor are upset both in storyline and in the technique—the camera angles which allow the spectator to see from the place of a number of different characters. But it can well be that myth, too, serves to confirm social distinction; in such a case, the spectacle of signs, a plenitude of significations, can serve as a rhetoric to proffer certain specific significations. Myth, as Barthes suggests, is fundamentally repetitive, stereotypical, the continued offering up of the same values. To avoid an obvious and self-damaging redundancy, myths can make use of the freeplay of signs as a guise of diversity; the different serves to mask the same. In the "Beautiful Girl" song in *Singin' in the Rain* (Stanley Donen, 1952), for example, we see a variety of women in different outfits, in different poses, in different color schemes. The effect is one of a visual richness; there is a lot for the spectator to see. But this richness works to overdetermine a set of mythic values which the film proffers: the woman as voiceless object (here the man sings to explain, to give a sense to, these women). What happens in such a scene is a proliferation of signifiers, but all of a particular kind, all tied ultimately to a single mythic system.

In this situation, myth and dispersion work together. But the systems of myth and dispersion can also exist as separate moments of a film and still work to the same end of political containment. Where the existence side-by-side of two systems in Fuller's films can have a critical force, because of the sharp break between them, in other films the transition between the two different uses of signs may be more fluid, less incompatible. In *Meet Me in St. Louis* (Minnelli, 1944), for example, Esther (Judy Garland) walks through the many rooms in her house and sings about "the boy next door" whom she is in love with. The camera follows her, moving in such a way as to signify little more than its virtuosity, its ability to present pleasant sights to our eyes; spectacle, as the continued presentation of sights, seems in full force. But, as if naturally, without premeditation, Esther and the camera arrive together at a window. We see Esther framed from outside by the window, converted literally into a picture of feminine beauty, a mythic object. Freeplay gives way to myth, but without obvious contradiction.

All this is to suggest that there is nothing inherently contradictory about a conjunction of myth and spectacle. Freeplay is an offer of signifiers which have no or too many signifieds; myth is an offer of signifiers which proffer a specific set of signifieds. Both processes, then are fundamentally and ultimately aspects of signification. Indeed, in a sense it could be said that spectacle itself is ultimately mythic. While its signifiers can serve no diegetic purpose, they still, in some way, signify: the function of spectacle is to signify itself, to signify the fact that it is art and not a believable image of a world. For all its rejection of particular moralities, the playfulness of Hollywood cinema, for example, is still a moral system, signifying to its audience that a playful approach to living is far more honest than other, more seemingly serious lifestyles. Both myth and spectacle can block intervention, praxis, activity, in the real complexity of the social world, by offering compromise relations to that world: myth by freezing certain values and repressing others, and spectacle by suggesting that there is no reality behind the richness of forms. Indeed, much of the inadequacy of structural/material cinema as a political cinema comes from the fact that it rejects one fiction—that of story and the values of myths—but remains nonetheless in the realm of another form of fiction: aesthetic activity itself as the only noncorrupt form of reality, as a substitution of forms for social realities. Structural filmmaker Malcolm Le Grice suggests that "work which seeks to 'portray' a reality existing in another place at another time is illusionist" and against the claims of illusionist cinema, he argues that "the only art which deserves to be called 'realist' is that which stems from the confrontation of the audience with the material conditions of the work" ("Paper at the London Film Co-op," 1976). But Le Grice fails to examine fully the nature of cinema as activity. There is a sense in which to do cinema at all, to try to work on the world through signifiers, is illusionist. Such an approach still sees reality as composed of separated subjects and objects, kept apart in the act of watching.

Christian Metz suggests that film, as signifier, is an imaginary form, unreal and alienating in its presentation of images, there, to an audience, here. Independent of content, the art of cinema presents to its spectators a closed production, mere substitutes, for activities that are elsewhere, beyond significations. The extreme version of Sartre's "present absence," the cinema is absent to its spectators in two ways: as a representation of events from an irretrievable past, and as a presentation in a viewing situation that preempts activity through a conversion of possible other interactions with the world into the simple activity of watching signifiers. The cinema is, therefore, present in only one way—as an alienation. The cinema is an unreality in the midst of reality.

This is not to suggest that a political cinema would therefore be one that went beyond fictions to present events directly; the very fact of cinema is a fiction. The reality of things cannot be signified; as Barthes argues in his self-critical work, "denotation is only the last of connotations" (*S/Z*, p. 16). Historical reality, and this is the point of my argument so far, is not a mere signified, a content to be seized up by cognition; what cognition knows is not historical reality, but a reification of it, a freezing, what Sartre will call a "totality" as opposed to the practice of "totalization," of history in motion. History is an activity in process, giving no fixed place, no final identity to knower or known. History is not objects out there which we know, but practices which we make, and which make us.

To work with signifiers is fundamentally to put oneself in a symbolic relation to historical process. Even if one rejects signifieds of content, one can still remain in the realm of signs; as Barthes argues, "Representation is not defined directly by imitation: even if one gets rid of notions of the 'real,' of the 'vraisemblable,' of the 'copy,' there will still be representation for so long as a subject (author, reader, spectator, or voyeur) casts a *gaze* towards a horizon on which he cuts out the base of a triangle, his eye (or his mind) forming the apex" ("Diderot, Brecht, Eisenstein" in Barthes, 1977, p. 69). To watch a minimalist film is still to watch a film *there*, on the other side of a line in front of a spectator. Representation in art, then, mirrors what Marx saw as occurring in that form of historical understanding which reified the past (and so could never move beyond mechanically repeating it): regardless of content, representation, in whatever area of human practice, works to put subjects and objects in two different spaces, both frozen, blocked from history. Le Grice's theory of cinema, for example, may banish story and character, but it significantly repeats the basic reification of entertainment cinema: spectators outside an activity which they watch. (Revealingly, Le Grice allows the whole apparatus of signification to return in his theory: "[There] is the need for the issue of 'content' to be applied to 'form.'... Signification of the so-called 'form' is at least as necessary a critical approach as that of the signification of the image and action"—op. cit.)

Le Grice's film practice, though, exhibits moments in which the activity of film goes beyond signification and representation as the separation of subject and object. In these fugitive moments, a new practice of cinema, one which involves a necessary activity beyond watching on the part of the spectator, is called into force. In *After Monet* (1974), for example, Le Grice uses four projectors, and halfway through the presentation begins to jiggle one of the projectors, drawing the spectator and film into the immediate conditions of presentation. This is not yet materialist practice, for it confuses the immediate material reality of projection with its materialist reality as *social* event, but it does show a way in which one can introduce a *real time and place* beyond signification into the activity of film.

What cinema seems to need to be politically progressive is not to insert history into its texts, but to insert its texts into history.[45] In this way, cinema would address itself directly to the question we saw Walter Benjamin asking criticism to raise: what is the place of it *as* a social force, rather than the way it represents social forces. The reality of cinema is not just in what it represents but what it is: an interaction between text (intra and inter) and spectator. Cinematic practice which dealt with the reality of this interaction would not be one which showed things to spectators, but one which encouraged, even required, the intellective involvement, the conscious engagement of the spectator. Le Grice does this in an ahistorical way in *After Monet* but there is nothing to prevent films from working to involve viewers as historically specific beings in the production of the meaning of a film. This strategy asks the spectator to evaluate his/her knowledge against the film; it reminds the spectator that meaning is really social meaning, dependent on the ways one decides to relate to history, including film as historical act. In this situation, the cinema is not a signifier but an open process, its meaning not there on the screen but in the spectator, through the spectator.

A standard political response to the ways in which regressive practice does not proffer political understanding, does not give voice to an understanding of history as struggle and contradiction, is to argue for a kind of documentary realism, a break through the mystifications and obfuscations of absence to make the not-said present. An extreme version of this faith in the power of the newly spoken to alter ways of seeing occurs in Godard's declaration in the 1960s that, as part of his political struggle through cinema, he would make a point of mentioning "Viet Nam" at least once in every film. I've suggested that any new knowledge may restructure the semiotics of a culture (see the discussion earlier of *All in the Family*), and the struggle to allow unheard realities a chance to speak—the struggle, that is, for *access*, as in current debates on media access—is undoubtedly an important one. But, as we have seen, any moment in a text is no more than one intratextual signifier, subject to displacement by differences in the text and by the relation of that text to the whole social text of a culture's meanings. The effect of these two forces on the signifying power of specific signifiers may be a containment, a distortion, of voice. Viet Nam can always be mentioned; the question is how. For example, in *Yours, Mine, and Ours* (Melville Shavelson, 1968), the war in Viet Nam is used as a symbol of completeness, of ultimate sense; in this story of a widow (Lucille Ball) and widower (Henry Fonda) who, with eighteen children between them, decide to marry, it is the drafting of one of the sons that helps bring the two families together, reconciling differences in the face of a higher duty.

Very different from this containment of meaning is what happens at the end of Vera Chytilova's *Daisies* (1966). Here we see two women, in loving detail, destroy a banquet: they fling food, walk on the platters of food, and smear food on the walls and on the tablecloth. This scene suddenly gives way to documentary footage of war events followed as suddenly by an end title which reads something like: "This film is for those people who were more outraged by the destruction in the banquet scene than they were at the war footage." In an extreme—perhaps too extreme—way, this scene, another fugitive moment in a film which otherwise luxuriates in *showing* events, represents a practice of cinema which is beyond showing and telling, and into involving. Not merely bringing war into the film—as Godard talks of doing—as a mere signifier, *Daisies* plays a signifier off against another signifier across the intratext of the film *through* the necessary judgement of the spectator. This intratextual play calls into question both a social myth (that war is not to be known, that it must remain unspoken) and, more importantly, a certain quality of cinema as spectacle and dispersion. The banquet scene doesn't say anything—it is just there to be watched in its spectacular meaninglessness—but the intervention of the spectator, encouraged by a particular strategy in the film, makes the scene reveal something both about human actions (that every action, like that in the banquet scene, has its value relative to other social actions) and about the specific cinematic representations of human actions (that cinema can inconsequentially and very easily represent the inconsequential).

The following pages try to set out some of the practices in a cinema and criticism of involvement—a practice which works to be *dialectical* in its possible interactions of text and spectator, in its implication of the spectator in the text. We will first consider the theory of Sergei Eisenstein, who moved toward an encompassing rhetoric of persuasion in film—a cinema which could move the spectator from mere observation of a world to a conceptual, political knowledge of the world and from there, without break, to action in that world. Next, a metacommentary on the American avant-garde will show how a reading can add a socially critical edge to a cinema that has all too often been read as the triumph of the asocial, the completely aberrant. The following chapter will examine the distantiation theory of Brecht, in which spectators, by criticizing typical representations in theater, would learn to criticize the typical representations of their lives. Finally, as a coda, we will consider the work of Nagisa Oshima in several of his films (most especially *Realm of the Senses,* 1976), in which the lack of political awareness by characters—their inability to totalize experience—encourages political awareness in the spectators—an awareness of where the characters are in history but also of where the spectators are. In these quests for a cinema that would truly be a practice of cinema and a cinema of practice, we are in contact with a new role for understanding, now given a critical, intervening, practical function. Such an art, in going beyond poesis, beyond signification, indeed beyond art, might well realize the function Marx assigned to a new mode of being and acting in the world. Whereas, as Marx suggests in "The Eighteenth Brumaire," past historical understanding was mere repetition no matter how political its content, the practice of cinema *as practice*, as production, can break through repetition and reification. As Marx says, "[in past revolutions] form went beyond content, here content goes beyond form."

2

Eisenstein as Theorist

To think is to generalize.

Eisenstein, "Montage 1937"

[My film] of *Kapital* will be dedicated—officially to the 2nd
International. The formal side is dedicated to Joyce.

Eisenstein, "Notes for a Film of *Kapital*"

We are still far from understanding the work of Sergei Eisenstein. Despite the
increased availability of authoritative versions of his finished films (and, now,
constructions of the aborted *Bezhin Meadow* and *Que Viva Mexico*), and
despite major efforts, in translating and publishing, to make his voluminous
writings known outside the Soviet Union, the text "Eisenstein" is still
ambiguous, contradictory, undecidable. It is yet to be interpreted.

Most surprisingly, there has been little effort to relate Eisenstein's own
work to a Marxist theory of art, and specifically to a theory of an aesthetic
dialectic. In some cases, a scholar, working from a sharp definition of what a
political film is or might be, and of what realism is (often as assimilation of the
category of the political and of the realist to a kind of "documentary realism")
has contained Eisenstein within the limits of that definition. This, for example,
would appear to be the case with the discussion of Eisenstein in Dudley
Andrew's *The Major Film Theories* (1976) where Andrew's initial division of
film theory into formative (formalist) and realist traditions makes it difficult
for him to situate political art. Unable to conceive the ways in which a theory
like Eisenstein's rejects the categories of formalism and documentary realism
alike, Andrew can only go with his first impressions of the work of Eisenstein
and so put him in the formalist camp, a strange bedfellow for theorists of the
autonomy of art like Munsterberg and Arnheim.

In Andrew's discussion there is, to be sure, a recognition of the existence of
political aspirations in Eisenstein, since Eisenstein's concerns with cinema as a
new machine of the Soviet age are a trouble-spot for any interpretation which

would understand Eisenstein outside the political. Andrew's answer is ultimately to read Eisenstein as a kind of Romantic artist for whom such interests as politics become aspects, mere constituent parts with no enduring force of their own, of a broader organic and aesthetic theory. Still, Andrew at least acknowledges the problem. There are (many) other critics who present Eisenstein's encounter with Soviet Marxism as a kind of accident; using such evidence as his pre-1917 sketches and drawings, critics will draw a continuous line between Eisenstein's pre- and post-revolutionary days.[1] They may even read Eisenstein's references to the political ends of art as evidence of an artist's needs to compromise and say what the state wants to hear.

Yet even when critics do pay attention to Eisenstein's constant reference to the ends of art, specifically the art of cinema, they often cast Eisenstein as the first or primary figure in purely rhetorical tradition—film as the production of calculated effects—but fail to examine the political context, the form and function, of such rhetoric. Eisenstein becomes a supreme and superb technician of the cinema, developing the most refined way to put pieces of film together. In *Theories of Film* (1973), Andrew Tudor, to take just one example, goes so far as to apply Eisenstein's five types of montage to an analysis of *The Wild Bunch* (Sam Peckinpah, 1969), ignoring Eisenstein's constant avowals that his theory of montage related to a (Marxist) way of representing *and* effecting political action. Eisenstein once more becomes a formalist, his discussions of film form pulled from the body of his text and made to fit wherever a critic wants.

In the last decade or so, of course, especially after French May '68, there has been a beginning attempt by radical film culture to discover antecedents for its practice, and this has led to a certain discovery of a political Eisenstein. Most important in this respect was the project of translation-with-commentary by the then Maoist *Cahiers du Cinéma* through the late sixties and early seventies.[2] But in the mid and late seventies, as *Cahiers* made a move back to a kind of romanticism of the artist and to a concern with artistic texts as expressions and embodiments of forms of desire, the presentation of Eisenstein changed; in recent work by *Cahiers* writers, Eisenstein becomes a kind of post-structuralist before his time. With his recourse to concepts of pathos and ecstasy—and their figuration in the orgiastico-religious explosions of *The Old and the New* (1928) and *Que Viva Mexico*—Eisenstein allows room for an interpretation of his project as an attempt to think out the pleasure of the text, of the freeing of signifiers from all critical ends. For example, for Jacques Aumont, the director of the *Cahiers* discovery of Eisenstein, Eisenstein's biography is essentially a kind of lived textuality, an endless taking up and playing with subject positions: Eisenstein's life is the constitution of a

writing [écriture]: writing which twists, which doesn't go straight ahead, pleasure of the text, of the drift, of what he calls calls "flanerie."... To write his autobiography is simultaneously bliss [jouissance] (of writing) and regression (he writes only of the symptomatic), *and* bliss of this regression itself. . . . The pleasure, constant, of scriptural drift is here multiplied by the bliss of pure memory . . . the textual work [travail], material body, the life, anamnesis. (*Montage Eisenstein,* p. 13)

One of the few texts to deal explicitly with the situation of Eisenstein in Soviet cultural politics is Peter Wollen's essay in his *Signs and Meaning in the Cinema* (1972); Wollen convincingly argues that Eisenstein's project only makes sense when one acknowledges and sorts out the myriad influences exerted upon him by his historical time. But Wollen's first interest in this chapter (and indeed throughout the book) is to establish the general conditions for a study of film as an art worthy of serious consideration. Wollen's particular discussions are thus confined to the level of an introduction, intended merely to establish the depth and complexity of film aesthetics; his Eisenstein chapter often seems a mere listing of names, as if Wollen wanted simply to show how the art of film in one historical situation was necessarily integrated with other arts and sciences of the time. Significantly, Wollen's postscript, added three years after the original edition, and which deepens the theoretical argument of the book, declares the Eisenstein chapter now to be the least significant of the three chapters.

There is a space open for political discussion of Eisenstein as a political artist. Without attempting to write away the contradictions of Eisenstein's work, I want to suggest in the following pages a reading of Eisenstein's theory of film as a Marxist theory. This discussion will be an experiment in the very strict sense: in this case, a hypothesis (Eisenstein as Marxist) applied to an object (for reasons I will clarify, Eisenstein's *writings*) to see what kind of match (or mismatch) ensues.

For a Marxist thinker, the initial impression of an object is not yet a perception of the historical value of that object. Dialectial understanding, based on the initial separation of objective reality and a human awareness of that reality, and on the possibility of an overcoming of that separation through practice, must be invoked to bridge the gap beteen the specific facts of actuality and the (historical) processes that structure actuality's concreteness. For Marx, "science would be superfluous if there were an immediate coincidence of the appearance and reality of things" (quoted in Lukács, "Writer and Critic," p. 26).

The lack of such a coincidence is quite relevant to the study of Eisenstein's aesthetics, and it may well be that the full import of Eisenstein as theorist cannot be grasped without an understanding of dialectics as an interaction of the concrete fact and historical process. Indeed, in an ironic fashion, it is the very inability of historians and theorists to go beyond their own first impressions of the implications of Eisenstein, and the resultant reification of these impressions as the concrete meaning of Eisenstein's project, which has led to the obfuscation of his importance in the history of cinema and of cinema theory.

The general confusion over Eisenstein appears to result, to a very large extent, from his work as a writer about film becoming confused with his work as a maker of film. Certainly, Eisenstein tried to link these two activities. His writing was intended, in considerable part, as an explanation and justification of his filmmaking; his writing would serve as the theory for his practice. (His writing was often undoubtedly motivated by another and more immediate tactical intention: to exculpate his film practice—to explain the *scientific* foundation of his films—in the face of an ever increasing socialist realist mentality in the Soviet Union.) Thus, Eisenstein prefaces *The Film Sense* with a quote from Delacroix in which there is a call for a merging of the creative and critical process, and throughout the book, justifies his theoretical arguments by reference to his artistic career. For instance, before talking about the acting experience as based on a sort of montage, he feels obliged to declare that his comments are derived from "observations of this 'actor's share' in my own work" ("Words and Image," *FS*, p. 37).

Yet Eisenstein's writings are more than a justification of his films— although they are certainly that. In his essays, Eisenstein attempted to evolve a general aesthetics of film (and an aesthetics of art in general, with the cinema discussed as the most advanced case)—both a synchronic aesthetics (film's role at a particular historical moment) and a diachronic one (film as the culmination of the aspirations of art). Film, properly used, would stand as the most splendid and highest illustration of major tendencies in cultural and humanist development. That Eisenstein saw his own films as major steps in this proper use of film's potential does not detract from a pressing need to begin a study of his broader theory of film.

It would of course be necessary to relate Eisenstein's film theories to his film practice for a complete understanding of his contributions to the art of film, but a more immediate need is that of rescuing him from the extremely one-sided emphasis on his *directorial* ability that has dominated most investigation of Eisenstein down to the present. Nothing might seem more concerned with form, with the freeing of techniques from any ulterior end, than the films of Eisenstein. But this first impression may well be based on a limited definition of realism. Separated from his theory—or with the theory seen as no more than an adjunct to the film production, so that values "uncovered" in the films are then read onto the theory—Eisenstein's film practice has seemed inordinately iconoclastic, and film analysts have tended to see in his films the triumph of an *un*realism, a formalism (foremost among these interpreters, of course, were the socialist realists).[3] His films suggest at first glance an extreme and elaborate departure from probability: stone lions move about, bicycle wheels spin wildly in a context-free space, objects and images literally dance, and in fact, all coordinates of space and time are juggled and jumbled. But none of this is necessarily in opposition to a conception of realism (one which, I will argue, Eisenstein held) as a conceptualization and, in some way, transcendence, of brute facticity. Central to Marxist thinking is a distinction between the apprehension of facts in their unmediated presentness, and an encounter with a history which cannot merely be cognized, confronted, seen, but which must be produced. Significantly, Eisenstein declared himself throughout this work to be a realist, consigning documentary to the realm of falsehood for its inability to do more than reflect (and inaccurately) the mere surfaces, the not-yet-historicized actuality of things. It may well be necessary, in fact, to re-look at Eisenstein's films themselves as examples of a *non*documentary realism.[4]

Much of the impetus for the miscomprehension of Eisenstein's work can be traced back to André Bazin, the dean of French film criticism. Bazin was a devoted analyst of film—devoted in a quite literal way since his epistemology of film was grounded firmly in his metaphysics, a peculiar brand of Personalist Catholicism—and he embarked upon his dichotomization of the cinema into realistic and unrealistic (an opposition which had the values of "good faith" and "bad faith") with a strong sense of mission.[5] Bazin took one aspect of film—its potential indexicality—and declared that in it resided the very ontology of film. An attitude, under the influence of a theology, was elevated into a law. For Bazin, the world, its objects, is a *text* as it were (although a text without coding),[6] an act of communication whose information can best be extracted if, as Bazin's value system has it, the recording instruments achieve a kind of transparence, a noninterference with the voice of the message. The world and its reflection in the human arts exist for Bazin in an asymptomatic relationship, art effacing itself ever further to approach Logos. (Bazin saw *Bicycle Thieves* as tending toward a condition in which there would be "in short, no more cinema.") Montage, the fragmenting of a pre-filmic world by a specifically filmic technique, is the enemy according to Bazin's theory, a necessary evil in pre-sound days but quickly replaceable in the evolution of cinema.[7]

Bazin's influence on subsequent film theorizing was immense. The dichotomy was applied anywhere and everywhere. Real versus unreal: there was little sense of the limitations of this opposition. The entire development of film was rewritten as a development of two opposed tendencies beginning with Lumière, the realist, and Melies, the unrealist, the magician.[8] Even those critics who countered Bazin did so polemically, by staying within the terms of his opposition.

In his article "The two types of film theory" (*A Critique of Film Theory,* 1980), for example, Brian Henderson discusses what he sees as two dominant forms of film theory—in Henderson's reading, the reflection theory of Bazin, and the part-whole theory of Eisenstein—and he insists on a clear, unbridgeable demarcation between the two theories. Bazin is, for Henderson, that theorist who has claim unequivocally to a theory of the real (which art reflects). Eisenstein is said to have no interest, except perhaps a dismissive one, in that problem, and instead directs himself to the more textually internal question of how parts go together in a film. Certainly, Henderson makes substantial criticisms of both Bazin and Eisenstein, but his reading (and evaluation) of Eisenstein is determined through his reading of Bazin on Eisenstein, and through Bazin's definition of reality as something that exists only on a reflectable level. For example, Henderson quotes with obvious approval Bazin's declarations that in the films of Kuleshov, Gance, and Eisenstein, "there is an abstract result whose origins are not to be found in any of the concrete elements." In fact, Henderson's comment, at least in regard to Eisenstein, is only partially correct: for Eisenstein, the result of montage would lead to something not to be found in the concreteness of objects in the image, but this something was not completely divorced from the concrete. For Eisenstein, actuality is contigent, ambiguous, polysemous. Montage, when properly used—when determined, that is, by a dialectical understanding of the dialectical nature of objective reality—would produce the general (historical) truths which structure the actual, the individual fact. The concept—what Eisenstein refers to as "imaginicity"[9]—is a mediation of images by their contextualization and their sense; it explains the real nature of their facticity. Thus, contrary to Henderson's definition of realism, Eisenstein always argued for a necessary connection between part-whole theory and reflection-theory as the only path to realism; only through the combination of nonsignificant (nonsignifying) parts into a meaningful whole would art be able to transmit and provoke the significance of the actual. In fact, Eisenstein and Bazin agree that objective reality possesses a meaning that can be reflected in art. For both, interpretation was a necessary antecedent stage to the presence and presentation of meaning. Eisenstein and Bazin disagreed merely over the stage at which interpretation occurs.[10] For Bazin, the world interprets itself (inspired as it is by the sense of God), and the recording medium of art serves a primarily phatic function, to ensure communication and maintain the channel.[11] For Eisenstein, in contrast, it is the filmmaker who must intervene and interpret an actuality that can't speak its own significance and which indeed tends to repress a real significance by a brute, dominating facticity, by the seeming evidence of the image.[12]

By equating the actual and the real, Bazin was reiterating the belief central to personalism that the objects of concrete actuality are an expression of a divine Logos that can be read by those followers who possess faith. Moreover, personalism took the form of a democratic theology: the Logos would speak to anyone who had faith, so that the intercession of priestly authorities would be unnecessary. Bazin's discontent with active intervention by filmmakers, and the distance he took from *la politique des auteurs,* was precisely an attempt to refute a priesthood of film. For Bazin, following Emmanuel Mounier's precepts, nature ideally provided its own interpretation, the surface of objects themselves having a direct link to, and serving as a reflection of, the divinely inspired *vie intérieure* of nature. Thus, Bazin called for an essentially passive role for film production; the cinematic genius was to be no more than the person who had the best intuitive understanding of the best ways (for example, the most revealing camera angle) by which the cinema could be used to reflect. Eisenstein, on the other hand, saw significance as a mere potential within concrete objects and images; although governed by an order, objective reality appeared, at first glance, chaotic, without logic. The filmmaker would intercede, would assume a necessarily active role as an interpretant: the filmmaking process is defined by Eisenstein as "a characterization—a definition of the represented matter" (*FF*, p. 52). If this interpretation was based on the precepts of historical materialism, this definition of primary material would come closest to approximating historical truth. For Eisenstein, materialist analysis was a path to truth which could express itself through the intermediary of the filmmaker, a worker who changed raw material. Indeed, if Eisenstein saw the role of film technique as one of abstracting from a specific actuality, a similar process was necessary for the filmmaker as individual, as a specific self who had to abstract him/herself from his/her actual, and therefore limiting, point of view. Eisenstein's obsession with learning, with immersing himself in all the currents of human thought, may well be read as his attempt to rise above the limits of his situation to a larger cultural view in which one does not speak in one's personal voice but in the voice of history. Materialism served in this project as the master model, the organizing framework. Jacques Aumont aptly notes that Eisenstein very much saw art as having a social content—namely, its representation and production of a course of human history—and he explains that "this verité of content—always more or less relative to the author and his/her arbitrary—had no chance to be the 'authentic' unveiling of reality unless this author based him/herself on 'the positions of the working class'" (Aumont, p. 188, quoting Eisenstein, *Montage, 1937*).

In his theory then, Eisenstein distinguished two levels of objective reality, one less real, mediated by the other: the filmmaker was to manipulate one level, the actual, to reveal its *necessary* connections to the other level, the determining real course of human history. Yet Eisenstein saw nothing idealist or subjectivist in this manipulation: the connections brought forth by the artistic perspective were connections with a real existence in an objective reality anterior to and outside the intervention of the filmmaker, but uncoverable by the filmmaker since these were connections which implicated the filmmaker's own historical situation. Eisenstein's theory is not subjectivist, then, since the artist does not create meanings *ex nihilo,* but produces them from a nature that is non-indifferent.[13] The theory is not, on the other hand, idealist since it is only in material practice—in the active intervention of a filmmaker, for example—that a non-indifferent nature can overcome the indifference of facticity; historical understanding is not teleological, a voice that will inevitably be heard, but a possibility that a worker such as the filmmaker must help to realize. The first stage in such a dialectical understanding of the structure of reality is the recognition that this organization exists outside of that understanding and can only be comprehended through work. Eisenstein refers constantly to a logic of objective reality: the filmwork must participate in this logic. Eisenstein prefaces one of his most important essays, "A Dialectical Approach to Film Form" (*FF,* pp. 45-63) with a quotation from Razumovsky's *Theory of Dialectical Materialism:* "According to Marx and Engels the dialectical system is only the conscious reproduction of the dialectical course (substance) of the external events of the world." The success or failure of a film project is to be based on the accuracy of this reproduction, measured, of course, against the standard of Marxist history—history as conflict which works to transcend its conflictual nature.[14] The problem of pure formal experimentation, as Eisenstein sees it in the films of Vertov, is its inevitable inability to offer anything but sheer conflict, a play of forms. Thus, for example, Eisenstein castigates the montage pattern in Vertov's *Eleventh Year* (1928) for a one-sided emphasis on a metrical montage (that is, the simplest form of montage) "mathematically so complex that it is only 'with a ruler' that one can discover the proportional law that governs it" (*FF,* p. 73); at the same time, he praises *Potemkin* for its classical unity and its *organicness.* It is indeed organicity that guides Eisenstein's Marxism; what is in a reified world separated into the categories of pre-filmic actuality, artistic intervention, and audience effect, could become in a perfect situation a harmony in which no one element could be distinguished from any other. If Eisenstein's theory, with its imagining of cinematic utopia, is romantic and organic, as Dudley Andrew suggests, it is the romanticism and organicism of a *Hegelian* Marxism in which differences dissolve away under the force of a unifying system. Struggle leads to the end of struggle, subjects and objects finally come together in a posthistorical state: "Our montage is no longer the *struggle of contrasts,* giving an image to and reflecting class struggles; it is the reflection of *the unity of these contrasts,* giving an image to the end of this struggle by the suppression of classes, by the structuration of a society without classes..." ("Dickens, Griffith, and The Film Today," *FF,* pp. 235-56). Eisenstein's theory itself reflects the central problem of Marxist thought: its desire to be both a theory of "endless matter everywhere in motion" (Engels) and a truth value holding history in place by a coming-to-consciousness of the subjects of history (Lukács et al.).

Marxist aesthetics has, of course, often acknowledged a formal accuracy—an accidental but essentially correct analysis of the conflictual nature of objective history—in non-Marxist systems of understanding. Lukács's strong admiration for Balzac, for example, was based on a belief in Balzac's accidental accuracy in depicting matters of class without possessing consciously a class consciousness. Eisenstein also admitted that there was a certain value to earlier formulations of the relationship between particular and historical, or between object and sense. In "Structure, Montage, Passage," for example, he cites Ignatius Loyola's visions as an example of an early *idealism* in which "there is said, openly, directly, and without circumlocutions, everything which is useful to our propositions" ("Structure, Montage, Passage," p. 21). Loyola claimed, as Eisenstein explains it, to have seen the essence of the Father more than the Father as essence; in other words, he had gone beyond corporeal embodiment to the values which give meaning to that corporeality. Insofar as Loyola saw the need to escape superficial impressions to strive for something more meaningful, his idealism bears a certain similarity to Eisenstein's project of recapturing a real through what at first seems an abstraction. But what Eisenstein sees as separating his work from such an idealism is its emphasis on the observer's own reality in this process of abstraction; the participant in the process of meaning-making doesn't merely watch, as Loyola would suggest, a logic going on elsewhere. Rather, the participant is part of that process, serving as both its cause (the active intervener) and its goal (to intervene, one must go through a dialectical process of transcendence of the shortcomings of individual perspective). For Eisenstein, meaning is a human practice. The final criterion of any attempt at historical materialist understanding will be its realization, or not, in practice; according to Lenin, "from active observation to abstract thought and *from there to practical activity*—such is the dialectical path of apprehending truth and objective reality" (quoted in Lukács, "Writer and Critic," p. 27, my emphasis). In Eisenstein's aesthetic, knowledge and action merge in the notion of *pathos*.

Pathos, for Eisenstein, is an empathetic projection by the perceiver of a work of art, but one which ultimately goes beyond empathy or projection—still essentially specular processes—to a more physically engaged activity. Through its affect—an affect organized and, in some sense, determined by the objective reality preexisting the filmwork—the work of art takes control of the viewer's perceptive functions (physiological and, hopefully, intellective) until that spectator begins to *act* in consonance with the logic of objective reality. The spectator loses his/her actuality, or, rather, transcends it in a process of incorporation; the film, already an act of abstraction, incorporates the spectator into this abstraction, gives the specific spectator a place in a broader process. Each spectator is first of all a specific person. However, by infection, the artwork will efface specificity, strip the viewer of his or her personal idiocyncracies, and will thus reveal his or her place as a participant in the process, the history, of human reality. As Eisenstein explains, "*pathos* . . . is that which makes one applaud and cry. In short, it is everything which puts one 'outside of one's self.' In other words, it could be said that the activity of *pathos* proper to an artwork involves bringing the spectator to *ecstasy*. *Ex-stasis* literally means 'going outside of one's self' or 'going outside one's usual state'"

("Structure, Montage, Passage," pp. 17-18). Yet, not all manifestations of ecstasy, of the going outside of one's self, are desirable. Eisenstein's argument is for a directed, determined ecstasy; in his conception of the historical dialectic, the only tolerable pathos-filled projection would be that in which *ex-stasis* grew organically out of the dialectical double-articulation of reality and art. According to Eisenstein, "as a prototype for a pathos-filled construction, one uses the same formulae by which the very movements and vitality of the phenomena of reality are produced" (ibid.). Or, as he declares elsewhere, "the very nature of montage not only ceases to be divorced from the principles of *realistic* film delineation but serves as one of the most coherent and practical resources for *realistic* narration" ("Word and Image," *FS,* pp. 10-11, my emphasis).

What I have referred to as the double articulation—and the invocation of linguistics here is deliberate—in both the processes of objective reality and of film in inserting itself into that reality and then enabling its fruition, is of central importance in Eisenstein's work. It is the very possibility that the articulations of film and of history can coincide, as Eisenstein's use of the quotation from Razumovsky suggests, that makes film a most appropriate art for a materialist aesthetics. Just as in reality there is an inertness which is rendered dynamic by the *process* of history, so Eisenstein sees in the cinema a hierarchy, or a dialectic, of the polysemous single image, and the unicodical interpretation which the image undergoes in montage. The cinema is a metonymy of historical processes, but also, and necessarily, more than a metonymy, since its interventions are one of the motors of that history. The single image, for Eisenstein, has as its referent the polysemous surface of objects and, because of its recognizable and familiar nature (its photographic actuality), the spectator seems to be pulled naturally toward that referent, taking the actual for the real. There is a propensity to confuse perceptually the look of things with the sense of things, and the naturalism of film's indexicality exploits this confusion. This propensity is no doubt connected to an economy of energy: it is easier, less demanding, to accept things as they appear to be. The spectator accepts an image that conforms to habitual perceptions. William Earle, in his essay "The Revolt Against Realism in Film," pinpoints the confirming power and appeal of belief in the meaningfulness of objects in their initial appearance: "Existentially, the satisfactions of realist [sic] art most seem to be created precisely in order to extinguish the lurking anxiety that the real world is nothing in the first place but a delusive fiction."[15] Eisenstein's dialectical distinction of actual and real leads to a historical understanding of this cultural—in Earle's words, existential—propensity. By confirming initial impression, the indexical image tends to lead to a confirmation of the nature being presented. It is ideologically advantageous in particular historical situations for people not to question the validity of initial impressions, and for the coded status of these impressions to be unnoticed. As Eisenstein states in his essay "The Cinematographic Principle and the Ideogram" (*FF*, pp. 28-44), "the representations of objects in the actual (absolute) proportions proper to them is of course merely a tribute to orthodox formal logic. A realism [documentary realism or actualism, I think he means here] is by no means the correct form of perception. It is merely the function of a certain form of social structure" (pp. 34-35).

The tendency of the photographic or cinematographic image to restrict perception to the perception of actuality established film as the major artistic battleground for the problem of double articulation, since the very indexicality of film propels it more than any other art towards an undialectical view of the actual. In expressing the need for a critique of film's naturalization of the cultural, Peter Wollen has suggested that "Godard's work is particularly important for the cinema because there, more perhaps than in any other art-form, semiological mystification is possible. . . . The cinema seems to fulfill the age-old dream of providing a means of communication in which the signals employed are themselves identical or near-identical with the world which is the object of thought" (*Signs and Meanings*, p. 165). Whereas Godard sets out to demystify the image by techniques of self-reflexivity, Eisenstein proposes to make the image a mere building block in a very different discourse than the one of that image itself. Both Godard and Eisenstein recognize the culturally determined propensity of the merely actual toward a mythology of the natural. Insofar as it masks its codical determinations, the film image thus represents for Eisenstein the greatest artistic challenge to dialectical art.

"At the intersection of Nature and Industry stands Art," answers Eisenstein ("A Dialectical Approach to Film Form" *FF*, p. 46). The artist intercedes to give direction to the initial directionlessness of actuality. Art makes Nature productive. The naturalistic image doesn't speak, or, more precisely, it only speaks the historical incompleteness of its recording of mere surfaces. Montage makes an image speak: "A single fragment of meaning equals a minimum of two fragments of a montage. One fragment is *not, after all, visible;* the first fragment is used for surprise, the second for perception" ("Notes for a Film of *Kapital*," 1, p. 13).

Film is, furthermore, an attractive art for political intervention, since the very appeal of film as a "natural" medium is an appeal that can be utilized by the dialectical artist to trick audiences virtually into believing that they are seeing the same old naturalistic art. By "naturalizing" the montage structure, by not calling attention to its "unnatural" status as a result of conscious intercession, and, most important, by using the mathematically calculated affective pull of the montage pattern, the filmmaker presents his or her audience with a film that has, or seems to have, the same perceptual attributes as the most "unbiased" documentary. *"Potemkin,"* Eisenstein declares at one point, "looks like a chronicle or a newsreel of an event but it functions like a drama" (*FF*, p. 162).

Indeed, it was the very degree to which the first articulation of theater—its separate elements, its raw material of actors on a stage—already manifested a high degree of convention, of artifice, that impelled Eisenstein to move, as he put it, "through theatre to cinema." In his writings on the theater, one senses Eisenstein's frustrations at working in a medium in which dialectical unity of actuality and reality is marred by the extent to which actuality itself is present only in a distorted form. At no level did theater present a minimal unit that could stand as an *analgon* for the natural; the theater was from the start an abstract art, but one with no transcendence. Whereas Eisenstein's filmwork could be based on a dialectical overcoming of the intense inclination of the film images toward the natural, and indeed could turn that inclination to its own advantage, his theater work had to first concern itself with reinvesting materiality back into the artwork. Given Meyerhold's influence on Eisenstein, this concern manifested itself primarily as a need to reassert theater's potential for physicality. Where theater could be most actual was in the brute here-ness of its staging as physical fact. In the Meyerhold theater, the physical, as in the outward nature of the actors in their rejection of Stanislavskian depth and introspection, was of prime importance; the influences on Meyerhold and, consequently, on Eisenstein, ranged from William James ("We don't cry because we are sad; we are sad because we cry") to American slapstick comedy. Out of this need to efface convention and symbolization, and promote the directness of the physical, arose Eisenstein's notion of typage; by calling for actors who "look the part," typage puts an end to the need for make-up, for a convention which masks particulars or, in fact, creates false particulars. Typage is the substitution of the actual for the professional. In his own theater work, as designer and later as director, Eisenstein continually emphasized the physical. The text became a mere pretext for a whole array of gymnastics. In *The Mexican,* for example, an adaptation of a Jack London story, Eisenstein staged a boxing match scene as a real fight: "real fighting, bodies crashing to the ring floor, panting, the shine of sweat on torsos, and finally, the unforgettable smacking of gloves against taut skin and strained muscles" ("Through Theatre to Cinema," *FF,* p. 7). Physicality was asserted to an even greater degree in Eisenstein's direction of Ostrovsky's *The Wise Man.* The play was staged as a three-ring circus and emotional states were rendered by a literal visualization of metaphors (for example, the double take of astonishment was expanded into an actual backwards somersault—a literal recoil).[16] In even further adherence to his belief in art as a series of carefully planned affects, several of the actors made their transitions between scenes by crossing a tightrope stretched above the audience (thus making audience fear a constituent part of the drama), and at the end of the play, fireworks exploded under the chairs of the spectators. Art became a set of shocks in the most literal sense.

Theater was, for better or worse, however, predominantely a convention-based art. The insertion of physicality into the theatrical production did not arise logically out of any strong connection between the theatrical process and the processes of history. In consequence, any such insertion was bound to appear as unmotivated, illogical, unreal. In "Through Theatre to Cinema," Eisenstein admits that "our pranks in regard to Ostrovsky remained on an 'avant-garde' level" (*FF*, p. 13). If theater maintained its conventionality—and it was impossible for it not to do so since, for Eisenstein, its ontological destiny was to be a convention-based art—it would contain little possibility for a dialectical understanding of a non-indifference outside the stage action. Traditional theater contained little that was extratheatrical; its nature was, as it were, too non-indifferent. If theater was filled with a physicality imported from without, the ontology of theater would be brought under attack, and the theater would cease to exist as theater. In fact, this happened to Eisenstein's production of Tretiakov's *Gas Masks*, which was staged in a real gas factory; the separation of conventional and actual was so great—and the propensity of the spectators for the actual so intense—that the machinery of the factories asserted its own physicality, and the theatrical elements lost their appeal. The factory dwarfed the play. Eisenstein describes what happened next: "the cart dropped to pieces, and its driver dropped into the cinema" ("Through Theatre to Cinema," p. 8).

The cinema, as Eisenstein saw it, was particularly appropriate for the materialist process argued for in a dialectical aesthetics; images had a direct connection to actuality, and their manipulation through montage could reproduce the manipulation of objects by the logic of history. Affect was the key to the unity of reality and industry; affect, if properly used, could bring the spectator into consonance with the "beat" of reality. In *Film Essays*, Eisenstein goes so far as to refer to affect as *"the content of the work"* ("The Method of Making Worker's Films" p. 17). To be properly used, the affect of montage had to be exactly calculated to ward off both ambiguity and precise but misdirected (i.e., nonmaterialist or apolitical) shocks. Eisenstein's hierarchy of the five methods of montage—the metric, the rhythmic, the tonal, the overtonal, and the intellectual—was a major step in his systematization of film's possibilities for calculated affect.

Each level of montage grew naturally out of a simpler level—a level, that is, with a correspondingly simpler affective response. Metric montage is the cutting together of images to create an effect solely by the length of each image. Rhythmic montage is derived from metric montage; here, cutting is based on the interaction of shot length and motion within the frame. In "The Odessa Steps" sequence of *Potemkin,* metric and rhythmic are intended to contrast: the cutting does not coincide with the motion of the Cossacks' feet on the steps, and this disparity intensifies the effective horror of the scene. Tonal montage refers to the dominant emotional sense—the tone—of a montage pattern, based on the totality of its elements. For example, as Eisenstein suggests, his

The Old and the New conveys the thematic difference between the values of old religion and the new Soviet farm through tonal montage: the whole of the sequence of the priests praying ineffectively for rain is dominated by stasis, by long shots, by ornate imagery, in contrast to the next sequence of Martha, a young Soviet, dreaming images of fertility in a montage filled with motion and explosive kinesis. Overtonal montage depends on secondary resonances from moment to moment, scene to scene.

Each of the first four levels of affect is connected to a corresponding type of pathos. Eisenstein expressed great delight, for example, in the effect which rhythmic montage had on audiences during one sequence from *The Old and the New:* as scythes moved back and forth on the screen, the audience members began to rock back and forth in their seats. Yet, as a simple reiteration and encapsulation of the pathos of historical process in these levels of montage, affect only involved audiences in a coincidence with, rather than a comprehension of, the dialectical course of reality. In his search for a more directly useful, powerful, and supraemotional effect of film, Eisenstein conceived of intellectual montage.

The first four levels of montage were based on an affective influence on the precognitive, preconceptual sense organs of the audience members. To be sure, there was a refinement in perception from level to level, but this refinement was no more than a successive sharpening of always subconscious reactions; in this part of his aesthetics, Eisenstein's dependence on Pavlov's theories of reflexology is of undeniable importance. In contrast to the affective forms of montage, though, intellectual montage seems not immediately connected to a theory of involuntary response; it is preconscious, and not unconscious. Eisenstein certainly tried to deny the presence of any break between intellection and precognition, but until his later notion of inner speech had evolved fully, he was unable to articulate the connections of intellectual montage to other montage methods; there was a major difference between pre-perceptive affect and apperceptive effect.

Eisenstein had come across the possibilities of a conceptual montage through his research into hieroglyphic and ideogrammatic language, which had culminated in his belief in the possibilities of a nondiegetic metaphor that could comment on the nature of the diegesis. The culmination of this discovery was to be the film of *Kapital* which would not merely have *Kapital* as its subject matter, but would duplicate the arguments of *Kapital* in the very figuration— the rhetorical processes—of the film. This would require a new kind of cinema, similar in its break with the past to Marx's break with idealist philosophy. Eisenstein declared, "The proclamation that I'm going to make a film of Marx's *Kapital* is not a publicity stunt. I believe that the films of the future will be found going in this direction (or else they'll be filming things like the *Essence of Christianity* from the bourgeois point-of-view!)" (quoted in Moussinac, pp. 28-29).

In intellectual montage the juxtaposition of two concrete images can lead to an abstract (although more real) concept not contained fully in either of the two images. For example, the massacre of workers juxtaposed with the butchering of a cow suggests that workers are being butchered *(Strike)*. Yet, to declare that conceptualization takes place within the mind of the perceiving subject would be to allow for ambiguity in the reconstruction of meaning, and so would separate the dialectics of production from the dialectics of reception and possibly lead to irresponsible effects of a film on its audience. An utmost necessity in Eisenstein's theory was that of economy, the need to affect an audience by the quickest possible means. Emotional montage seemed to offer this, but with no possibilities for conceptualization, for *articulated* response; the only way to such a response seemed to be through chance, through a hope that audiences would conceptualize the film in the desired way. The viewer had to be brought into consonance with the historical meaning of the actuality/reality, and this could really be accomplished only if the viewer was given as little chance as possible to interpose his/her own creative unconscious, his/her own actuality, into the already correctly articulated dialectic of the film text.

Affect—the gripping of a spectator and the attendant effacing of that spectator's own individuality—was the dominant drive behind the film project. As Wollen nicely points out, "In so far as he [Eisenstein] is interested in semiology, his kinship is not so much with Saussure and structural linguistics, as Christian Metz supposes, as with Charles Morris and his Behaviourist semiotic" *(Signs and Meanings,* p. 69). Morris distinguished three levels of semiotic process—the semantic, the syntactic, and the pragmatic—and he subordinated the semantic and the syntactic by suggesting that the success of a communication be judged by the effect on the intended addressee. A successful semiotic act is one which causes a person to respond in a desired way (Morris, *Foundations of the Theory of Signs,* 1938). Eisenstein's affective cinema is very close to this; the success of a film communication is to be based on a determined response and action elicited in a viewer. Yet the pragmatic does not banish the syntactic or the semantic. Since art's function is to reproduce the dialectics of human reality in and through dialectical action, the structure of the work—its syntactic arrangement—must be carefully governed to bring about not just any affect but, rather, the *proper* affect. Furthermore, since the proper affect should not come about accidentally, but must derive from an artwork *with definite ties to real, concrete images and objects,* a semantic level—a reference to reality as the context and sense of the artwork—is also necessary.

The problem of conceptual thought, though, is that it is not as economical, as direct, as a shock, and it does not necessarily manifest itself immediately in action. When Eisenstein was writing his essays, Soviet cultural life seemed to him to be flooded by the overwhelming interest of the masses in all sorts of art.

"It would seem that the relations to culture and cultural achievement had long since been altered among us here by the October Revolution. . . . Everywhere one finds attention, interest, *thrift*—an *economical* mastery of pre-revolutionary achievements" ("Film Language," *FF*, p. 109). Thus, the union of economy and affectivity also had a basis in the needs of the time; when Eisenstein was writing, there was a need for the most important of the arts to try to become also the most influential of the arts.

Some sort of intellection in viewer response would be permitted if it would take place in an immediacy. Eisenstein hypothesized the existence of such an immediacy: affectivity and intellection merge in the concept of *inner speech.* The most immediate source of the concept of inner speech was Boris Eikhenbaum's essay, "Problems of Film Stylistics" (*Screen,* 1974) and the research of A. Luria, a student of Vygotsky. Like the French impressionist film critics writing at the same time, Eikhenbaum saw film as a new kind of poetry, geared to bring out the photogenicness of the world. Eikhenbaum asserted that film was best suited, after its initial and temporary career as a mass art, to serve as a special, atypical language for communicating the "trans-sensuality" of objects—that is, a sense which went beyond that of the immediate physicality of objects into their poetic essences. Yet, Eisenstein and Eikhenbaum disagreed markedly over the nature of this trans-sense. For Eikhenbaum, following the formalist belief in art as a renewal of perception, film was best suited to bringing out the photogenic qualities of objects—that is, those qualities which give any object a capacity for a beauty that it does not at first appear to possess in habitual perception. For Eisenstein, on the other hand, objects possess a capacity not for beauty but for the revelation of their participation in the processes of human reality. The function of art is not merely to redefine perception but to use that redefinition in the service of a socially useful action.

Influenced by Levy-Bruhl's research on "primitive" societies, Eisenstein saw two stages in human language development: these two stages were related both structurally and genetically. Human language had originally been alogical, affective, sensual, imagistic. This was a primitive language which made little distinction between images and the objects represented by images—this unity is obviously the source of magic and voodoo.[17] Therefore, primitive language could be understood to invoke affinities between human creation (the image) and natural creation (the object) which might parallel the process of dialectics. According to Eisenstein, primitive language remained in the human being as a latent capacity. The language of film—a language which used images rather than symbols—would be particularly efficacious in speaking to that part of the human cognitive faculties which was used in the understanding embodied in prelogical thought. Since meaning was immanent in the structure of imagistic communication, the stage of interpretation, which was a distinctly second stage in rational discourse, would merge to a large extent with the initial act of perception and thereby lose any arbitrariness it might have. For

Eisenstein, this imagistic communication inherent in the dialectical use of film was an automatic, unambiguous communication.

It is not possible to be conclusive, however, about Eisenstein's recourse to the concept of inner speech, since he never completely articulated what he meant by that form of speech. (Aumont suggests that Eisenstein dismissed the notion when Levy-Bruhl similarly rejected it in his own work.) Certainly, though, his sketchy comments provide a certain sense of inner speech as a universal, immediate language in which particular and universal are seen to be closer than in conceptual language. David Bordwell, in his essay "Eisenstein's Epistemological Shift" (*Screen,* 1974), tries to argue that with the concept of inner speech, Eisenstein moved into a dangerous concern with subjective associationism and private languages. However, although Eisenstein doesn't provide enough information to judge totally the implications of his adoption of a concept of inner speech, it seems to me that he argued for an inner speech precisely because of its powers in overcoming the particular, the idiosyncratic, the private. Part of Eisenstein's shakiness with the concept of inner speech may well be the result of the concept's origin for him in the problem of *inner monologue.* Yet inner speech and inner monologue seem decidedly different. Where inner speech is posited as a language base common to all users (in pathos, all audience members become the same), inner monologue is an individual's internalization of social language, of nonprimitive language to his/her own ends.[18] The problems of representing the thoughts of inner monologue in a medium inclined toward presenting surfaces had come up during Eisenstein's scriptwriting for the film version of Dreiser's *An American Tragedy;* to present the inner confusion of Clyde as he thinks about murdering his mistress, Eisenstein resorted to a complex montage of sight and sound.[19] It may well be that in thinking of the structure of Clyde's thoughts as a confusion of emotions *specific only to Clyde,* Eisenstein, in his notion of inner monologue, had in fact brushed up against associationism and subjectivism. It is perhaps not insignificant that when James Joyce met Eisenstein, Joyce declared that either Eisenstein or Walter Ruttmann had to film *Ulysses* if it was ever to be brought to the screen, for it was precisely in Joyce's work that, Eisenstein felt, the very question of the subjectivity/objectivity of inner monologue/mythic speech was raised in the strongest and boldest fashion. But in Clyde's monologue, it is clearly established that this is a representation of a particular pattern of thought and not of inner speech as a shared language.

Eisenstein's concept of inner speech is clearly and intimately connected with the notion of economy or laconism, as Eisenstein himself refers to it. There is nothing in Eisenstein's writings to suggest that inner speech was in any way democratic, that it in any way allowed perceiver freedom. In fact, the only democratic element in Eisenstein's writings is his belief that any and every element of the film piece—the shot—can be part of a montage (though, as we have seen, Eisenstein was a bit undemocratic in his hesitancy to allow montage within the frame as much importance as montage of shots). Eisenstein derived this notion of a democratic signification after a very influential tour of the Soviet Union by the Japanese Kabuki theater. In the Kabuki theater, every element in the production is equally significant; there is truly a monistic ensemble, to use Eisenstein's phrase. Eisenstein says of the Kabuki actor that "directing himself to the various organs of sensation, he builds his summation to a grand *total* provocation of the human brain, without taking any notice *which* of these several paths he is taking" ("The Unexpected," *FF,* p. 21). In one of Eisenstein's most famous observations, he declares that in the ideal work of art the separate acts of "seeing" and "hearing" would merge in the act of *feeling.* Affect is an end reachable by any number of technical paths. That the different elements of expression were equally significant was necessary to ensure that at every moment a film would yield its full capacity for affect, that no element would be irrelevant to this process. This is most obvious in Eisenstein's discussion of the interior monologue sequence in *An American Tragedy,* in which vertical montage (the synchronic montage of picture and visual tracks) went so far as to exclude one or the other of the tracks at several moments. It must be noted, though, that Eisenstein did not view monism ahistorically. He was quite aware that the affective/significative potentials of certain elements in a work of art could be altered by a historical situation. Thus, although his interest in film's pluricodical nature led him into an almost symbolist concern with signification theory of music and of color—a veritable theory of correspondences—he was quite ready to admit the social basis of any particular signification. His long discourses on the color *yellow,* for example, can be read as so many attempts to find not the meaning of the color, but the meaning it has for a particular time and place.

Clearly Eisenstein's notion of the monistic ensemble has affinities with the formalist notion of *device,* for example as described for cinema by Viktor Shklovsky in his essay "Poetry and Prose in Cinematography" (in Bann and Bowlit, *Russian Formalism,* 1973). Shklovsky argues that the values or aspects (formal, semantic, contextual, etc.) in an artistic text are ultimately interchangeable, and can be used interchangeably for identical ends. In the last-minute rescues in Griffith's films, for example, resolution is carried out through every major code operant in the text: screen direction, shot length, level of the histrionics, and so on. More recently, textual analysis, such as that of Raymond Bellour, has suggested that a goal for the analysis of film texts is an appreciation of the means by which films reveal a parallelism of various codes—for Bellour, for example, the ways in which camera movement and narrative work together in the beginning of *Marnie* (Hitchcock, 1964) or *Psycho* (1960).[20] Eisenstein is saying something similar to Shklovsky and the textual analysts when he declares that in the structure of *Potemkin,* "the whole *method* of *exposing* the entire event likewise accomplished its leap; a narrative type of exposition is replaced (in the montage rousing of the stone lion) and transformed to the concentrated structure of *imagery*. Visually rhythmic prose leaps over into visually poetic speech" ("The Structure of the Film," *FF*, p. 171).

Yet, as I have suggested, in subordinating the semantic to the pragmatic, Eisenstein made it difficult for himself to establish an equivalence between affective and intellective expression in film. Ultimately, Eisenstein has to rely on a myth: his position rests on the needed real existence of inner speech. Disavowing the creative role of the spectator, Eisenstein thinks he has achieved objectivity, but the only validation of inner speech is its necessity in the conceptual framework of Eisenstein's theory, not in any real existence it might or might not have. Perhaps if he had not tried to rank semantic and affective levels in semiosis hierarchically, Eisenstein might have come closer to an aesthetics that could be equally emotional and intellectual. More recent theory and practice has embarked on such an equalization. Peter Wollen censures Eisenstein for disavowing further research into symbolic aspects of film, "the necessary beginning for any movement towards the establishment of paradigmatic sets, such as the Gods sequence in *October,* though, as Godard has since shown in *Une Femme Mariée* and *La Chinoise,* this was not a dead-end street at all" (*Signs and Meanings,* p. 69). It might even be more apposite to cite Godard-Gorin's *Vent d'Est* (1971), in which affective devices blend imperceptibly into socially critical devices: the viewer's affective response merges with, or becomes, a political response. The film opens with a man and a woman who, in due course, are revealed to be representatives of the oppressed, chained together in a gorge. The shot is held for about eight minutes with little action other than minor body movements. The affective result is a demand in the viewer for something to happen, for the stasis to be ended. In the course of the film, it is suggested that this can only happen when the man and woman come to an awareness of their situation and climb out of their symbolic gorge in an act of revolutionary defiance. The viewer asks for a change in the affective situation of the initial viewing experience, and the film answers that such a change can only be political in nature. Whereas Eisenstein could only achieve the symbolic by recourse to metaphors outside the spatial-temporal coordinates of the diegesis, Godard and Gorin manifest a plot which in itself is politically symbolic.

Despite minor points of contact, there is a major divergence between Eisenstein and the formalists. Although he shared their interest in linguistic research—especially in his examination of film's two articulations—Eisenstein is primarily a political rhetorician. Economy, Eisenstein's hero, is the precise enemy of the formalist theory of perception; it is the very need to do things quickly which has caused us to lose an appreciation of the reality of those things, the formalists claim. It is significant that both the formalists and

Eisenstein refer to Herbert Spencer's "The Philosophy of Style," but that the formalists quote him with disapproval while Eisenstein quotes him with approval. In "The Philosophy of Style," Spencer continually supports a utilization and cultivation of language as an economic and direct pathway to a content to be transmitted by that language. With Spencer, Eisenstein attacks whatever might interfere with the transmission. Arrested perception—such as the formalists argued for—would, according to Eisenstein, contain the danger of viewer freedom, and the potential disarming of the film's affective power. In his cinema, the viewer had to think as little as possible. This meant that a film had to have affect without any arrest.

It is revealing, in this respect, to compare Eisenstein with his contemporary, Dziga Vertov. Eisenstein's comments on Vertov are significant:

> I see an extreme necessity to underline a radical difference of principle, namely in the diversity of methods employed, between my work and Vertov's. . . . This is to say that *Strike* did not claim to come out of art, and this gives it its force. . . . Such as we conceive it, the work of art . . . is above all else a tractor which works to find a basis for psychology according to an orientation along class lines. . . . We do not need a Kino-eye but a Kino-fist! ("Sur la question d'une approche matérialiste de la forme," *Cahiers du Cinéma,* 1970).

Through his kino-eye, Vertov hoped to reorganize ways of seeing at the level of initial perception. For example, Vertov's *Man with a Movie Camera* (1929) is not just "about" aspects of work in Soviet life but is an act of work in itself for the spectator who must actively build the meanings of the film.[21] Vertov's film is a self-reflexive meditation on the codes of cinema; Eisenstein never intended cinema to make manifest its own concerns. Eisenstein, to a much greater extent, saw film as no more than a social means, albeit the most effective one, to a social end; in his essay "Soviet Cinema" in *Film Essays* he goes so far as to declare, with apparent approval, that the art of cinema "is in the same class as the metallurgical industry" (p. 25). Eisenstein was not concerned with a liberation of, or even a reflection on, the signifier within a filmwork. In his Hegelian Marxism, he merely argues that naturalism has no real signified but that an organic art does. Engaging in an important critique of one kind of representation, Eisenstein then loses that critique in another, rhetorically based myth of representation. His signifier is controlled by an intent to cause the viewer to get at a signified (if we can call affect a signified or a content as he did) in the best possible—that is, in the simplest and most economical—way. His is a theory of how to organize the signifier *as an expression of a signified.* It may be appropriate that after May 1968, Godard chose the name of his film group from Dziga Vertov, who had laid bare the devices of his cinema, instead of concealing them in an affective, subconscious and preconscious, and perhaps ultimately illusionist cinema of the type argued for by Eisenstein.

3

Political Vagaries of the American Avant-Garde

A text is less a monument than a battlefield.

Jeffrey Mehlman, *Revolution and Repetition*

Living is easy with eyes closed, misunderstanding all you see.
line from the Beatles' "Strawberry Fields," heard on the soundtrack to
Michael Snow's *Wavelength*

Marxist studies of avant-garde art have generally tended to concentrate on an essential difference, an inevitable otherness, which they impute to that art. But their discussion takes a curious turn when they attempt to define what the avant-garde is different *from:* their answer, a strange one for Marxism to be making, is that avant-garde art is somehow different from the social, outside the productive relations of society, a thing apart. For Lukács, for example, this difference is a negative one. As Lukács reads the increasing reification of human relations in literary depiction from Zola to expressionism to Beckett, avant-garde literature increasingly reveals its *decadence,* its unreality: "one inescapable consequence of an attitude hostile or alien to reality makes itself increasingly evident in the art of the avant-garde: a growing paucity of content, extended to a point where absence of content or hostility towards it is upheld on principle" ("Realism in the Balance," *Aesthetics and Politics,* p. 41). In contrast, and often with Lukács as his specific adversary, Adorno argues that precisely because art separates itself from social representation, it stands as a critique of that representation, giving evidence of a structural completeness and unity that contemporary culture cannot yet admit: "art does not provide knowledge of reality by reflecting it photographically or 'from a particular perspective' but by revealing whatever is veiled by the empirical form assumed by reality, and this is only possible by virtue of art's own autonomous status" ("Reconciliation under Duress," *Aesthetics and Politics,* p. 162). Significantly, both Adorno and Lukács join in a mistrust of present reality, which they see as a realm of the empirical, the superficial; what separates the two critics is little more than the fact that Adorno views the relationship of progressive art to the present as a utopian, future-oriented one (avant-garde art is the negation of the negation—the present as empty position—to create a new positivity), while Lukács looks backwards, seeing the present as a fall from a classic plenitude (traces of which show up in only a few lonely voices—the brothers Mann, for example). In both Adorno and Lukács, the present state of social reality is fundamentally poor, fundamentally untrue.

But, as Fredric Jameson suggests in his critique of Lukács's notion of the decadence of the avant-garde, there is a danger in the assumption of art's separation from the social in that such an assumption can quickly slide from an understanding of the conditions of *relative* autonomy to one of such a separation as total, of the social field having no effect on that magical realm of the aesthetic dimension:

> The concept of decadence is the equivalent in the aesthetic realm of that of "false consciousness" in the domain of traditional ideological analysis. Both suffer from the same defect—the common presupposition that in the world of culture and society such a thing as pure error is possible. They imply, in other words, that works of art or systems of philosophy are conceivable which have no content, and are therefore to be denounced for failing to grapple with the "serious" issues of the day, indeed distracting from them.... Modernism would then [once we realize that every text has a relation to a social context] be not so much a way of avoiding social content... as rather of managing and containing it, secluding it out of sight in the very form itself, by means of specific techniques of framing and displacement which can be identified with some precision. ("Reflections in Conclusion," *Aesthetics and Politics*, p. 202)

Elsewhere, Jameson describes this act of identifying framing techniques and displacement as a "metacommentary," an activity which understands aesthetic production as a symbolic act and, then, reads back from the symbol to the thing symbolized, namely the historical situation: "just as every idea is true at the point at which we are able to reckon its conceptual situation, its ideological distortion back into it, so also every work is clear, provided we locate the angle from which the blur becomes so natural as to pass unnoticed" ("Metacommentary," *PMLA*, 1971, p. 9). Such a position tends to read every work as, in some way, realistic, as connected to a real situation; what distinguishes works is simply the extent to which they provide this reading themselves—as, for example, Godard-Gorin's film *Tout va Bien* (1972), with its opening discussion of its own production, tries to do—or whether that reading must come from the outside, from the intercession of the critic: "what is wanted is a kind of mental procedure which suddenly shifts gears ... and turns the very problem into its own solution ... by widening its frame in such a way that it now takes in its own mental processes as well as the object of those processes" (ibid., p. 9).

It is a metacommentary that I propose to engage in in this section—specifically, a metacommentary on certain trends in the American avant-garde cinema. My aim will be in a sense to read the realism of such a cinema, to emphasize its sameness, rather than its difference, in relation to other social processes. What I will suggest (and this will follow from arguments I posit throughout this study) is that the myth of the avant-garde, the proclamation (both denunciatory and supportive) of its otherness, follows from a mistaken view of the social as being equivalent in nature to certain of its practices, specifically those of narrative and representation, so that whatever is nonnarrative or nonrepresentational is seen as *essentially* different. The problems of such a reductive equation are evident in Jameson's own analysis of modernist strategies in *Fables of Aggression,* on Wyndham Lewis. While Jameson's study does have the value of isolating specific figures of containment in Lewis's corpus, Jameson rests his understanding of the value of modernism here on a limited view of that social world in which modernism takes its place, and in consequence, the social thrust of modernism is distorted. It is realism, for Jameson, that is the bourgeois art-form par excellence; Jameson speaks of "the general situation of modernism as a whole, for which some older common-sense notion of 'reality' has become problematical, and with it, a traditional faith in the transparency of language and an unselfconscious practice of mimetic representation..." (p. 38).

Jameson's confusion, as with most explanations of the "difference" of modern art, comes from his assumption that modernism's declaration that other forms of activity have become problematic is an accurate declaration and not just one internal to the modernist ideology. Jameson's view of history (inspired by Weber's and the Frankfurt School's investigation of bourgeois rationality, and their tendency to see rationality, scientificity, as the end-all of bourgeois practice) is, like that of modernism itself, one of the monolithic spread of a noncontradictory capitalism whose primary form of symbolic expression is in mimesis, and in which contradiction or negation can only occur from outside in the form of truly marginal political realisms or hypercritical modernisms. Jameson, like the Frankfurt School, like modernist ideology, virtually equates capitalism and mass culture (or, more precisely, a myth of mass culture); as a consequence, the realization of a popular political art (such as the one Brecht called for)—indeed, even the postulation of such an art—becomes impossible. Critical realism, like modernism, can only become an outsider to history. Attesting to the way any realist, "analytical and demystfying symbolic act is then itself reincorporated into what Marcuse calls 'affirmative' or legitimating establishment culture, and its original sense disappears," Jameson concludes that "today the most vital contemporary 'realisms'—and there are few enough of them—draw their vitality from the marginality of their content, from their historical good fortune in having as their raw material social realities which the dominant culture has not wished to see, let alone to express" (p. 64). With critical realism having had the "good fortune" to become a marginal force, and with mass culture unmarred by any internal contradictions that would allow progressive practices to emerge from its midst,[1] the way is open for modernism to install itself in Jameson's text as *the* critical form, *the* challenge to dominant culture:

> ... *great* art distances ideology by the way in which, endowing the latter with figuration and with narrative articulation, the text frees its ideological content to demonstrate its own contradictions; by the sheer formal immanence with which an ideological system exhausts its permutations and ends up projecting its own ultimate structural closure. This is, however, precisely what we will observe Wyndham Lewis' work to do.... However embarrassing the content of his novels may be for liberal or modernist establishment thought, it cannot but be even more painful for proto-fascism itself, which must thereby contemplate its own unlovely image and hear blurted out in public speech what even in private was never meant to be more than tacitly understood. (pp. 22-23, my emphasis)

This process (and note how Jameson's words impute this process to the text and not to its reading), by which a text may be read to draw its ideological presuppositions to an extreme and ultimately self-critical position, may well be one that can be found in Wyndham Lewis, and Jameson's reading does make explicit certain ideological assumptions in Lewis's novels that would make any future reading a more politicized one. But the way Jameson understands his political reading obscures two points about that reading: first, that it is a reading; there is continually in arguments like Jameson's about the "inevitably" self-critical or self-subversive force of certain texts an attribution of this force to the text alone and not at all to the reading. Yet, obviously, any number of artists deemed to be subversive can be and have been read differently.

Jameson's localization at the level of the text of what is actually a practice between text and reader (and note how Jameson's reader is pictured outside history, outside class) feeds into the second problem of his position, which is visible precisely in his reference to great works of art: with this appeal to systems of value, to value *in* works, Jameson gives in to a whole framework of bourgeois aesthetics, in which any number of nonobjective sources of value (for example, taste, or the imposition of tradition) are confused with the objective relations of texts to their history.

There is nothing necessarily wrong with a desire to found a theory of value within a Marxist aesthetics. In reading the work of critics like Terry Eagleton or Jameson (here at least), however, one can't help but be struck by the ways in which their canons reduplicate the choices of the high art tradition. Indeed, Eagleton goes so far as to suggest that the valuation of great works by bourgeois criticism is an unconscious or preconscious awareness by the critic of the politically progressive nature of such works; Eagleton pictures the bourgeois reader as a proto-Marxist for whom the great works most forcefully stir the deeply embedded and often self-concealed wish for a different social system (*Criticism and Ideology*, p. 179).

The defense of modernist ideology is limited when it confuses one aspect of the aesthetic dimension with the whole of the ideological practice of that dimension, and fails to see how formalism—the foregrounding of technique as technique—can equally be part of traditional aesthetic practice. In the recent theoretical defense of avant-garde film practice, this problem can be traced most immediately to the influence of theories like linguist Benveniste's on the difference between *histoire* and *discours*, or between *enunciation* and *énoncé*.[2] Geoffrey Nowell-Smith's approving discussion of the terms clearly pinpoints what is at stake:

> Discourse and history are both forms of enunciation, the difference between them lying in the fact that in the discursive form the source of the enunciation is present, whereas in the historical it is suppressed. History is always "there" and "then," and its protagonists are "he," "she," and "it." Discourse, however, always also contains, as its point of reference, a "here" and a "now" and "I" and a "you".... The [discursive] film, therefore, can hold a discourse toward the spectator as that which exhibits itself to be seen, or for that matter, as that which enables the spectator to see.... Not only is exhibitionism, as Metz notes, "of the order of discourse, not of history"... it is also discursive articulation. History becomes discourse in so far as the exhibitionist/voyeur relation (...) presides over the construction of the film. ("A Note on History/Discourse," *Edinburgh 1976 Magazine*, p. 27)

Discourse, then, is a kind of inclusion or, in some cases, a restoration, of an enunciating instance to an *énoncé;* it is a reference, in phenomenological terms, to the intentionality (authorial and spectatorial) of an act of enunciation. It is the foregrounding of markers of enunciation in an art ostensibly devoted in its commercial forms to an unreflected *énoncé* that proponents of the avant-garde film see as the political accomplishment of such a cinema. For Pam Cook, for example,

> [In Michael Snow's *Wavelength*] it is through the spectacular display of *process* that the discursive comes about: the film exhibits itself as process and transformation, refusing the masquerade of history. It constructs the spectator as the one who is looking at the film, as the "you" addressed specifically and immediately, in a shifting relationship with the "he," "it," "there," and "then" which are held at a distance in a process of negation. ("Teaching Avant-Garde Film," *Screen Education Notes,* 1980, p. 87)

My suggestion that this theory of enunciation echoes phenomenology's emphasis on intentionality was deliberate, because it is precisely the extent to which the valorization of discursive markers, and of the project of self-reflexivity in general, is little different from the basic phenomenology of any communicative act, that shows up the imputed difference, the supposed modernity of modernism, as a guise, an attempt to deny continuities. A fundamental suggestion of phenomenology is that, at some level, every human action asserts its "hereness" and its intention as a communication from an "I" to a "you." In particular, the aesthetic dimension has as its engendering condition a recognition (by the art consumer) of its discursive nature—of, for example, a film's status as an act of entertainment and not really a believable presentation of a story "there" with characters like "him" and "her." The self-reflexivity of discourse is nothing new or unique. Indeed, Leo Spitzer's essay, "American Advertising Explained as Popular Art" (in *Essays on English and American Literature*) suggests that a reflection on the enunciating instance (like that imputed by Pam Cook to *Wavelength,* to cite only one example) may well be a source of the selling power of advertising *as bourgeois art.*

Spitzer, analyzing a Sunkist orange juice ad, notes that it tries not at all to hide discursive markers, making no claims to a realism: indeed, going so far as to create a glass of orange juice that is the same size as the sun, the ad clearly establishes itself as an aesthetic object (that is, it focuses attention on the "hereness" of its practice) and explicitly foregrounds the fact that it is a message from a seller to a buyer. The ad is permeated with an intentionality. It is "for you," and this flattery, the way it inscribes its reader into its activity, only increases its appeal. Indeed, extended attention on the part of the recipient to the rhetorical devices of the ad can increase respect for the ad, rather than deconstruct it; like a magic trick, the appeal of an advertising trick only increases the more we inquire into its discursive conditions of existence.

Metz's (and Nowell-Smith's) comparison of discourse to exhibitionism is a useful one, for it demonstrates political limitations of the *histoire/discours* distinction. There is a suggestion in the comparison that exhibition is a subversive act, that in breaking down the fourth-wall effect of realist art (Bazin's notion of film as a window on the world), film which asserts its "I" challenges the escapist tendencies of bourgeois art. But the assumption that bourgeois art is devoted to a "there," an elsewhere, is inadequate. Much of the entertainment value of a film derives precisely from the understanding that the film is "for you." (This may be one reason why cinema-verité has had no mass appeal. Cinema-verité goes out of its way to hide markers of enunciation—editing patterns, narrative, structure—and so violates the exhibiting contract normally agreed upon between film and spectator. For many people, cinema-verité seems to be a betrayal of fundamental conditions of cinema.) Exhibition is frequently part of the appeal of aesthetic practices.[3]

What the emphasis on restoring enunciation to art fails to realize—beyond the fact that art is enunciative—is that the political containment of art derives not from a repression of the marks of enunciation, of textual intentionality, but from a social base which is more than an "I" or a "you" or the "here and now" of the aesthetic act. Both discursive and historical art (if there really is an art totally of the historical) substitute for the understanding of art as a social activity a number of *alibi origins:* the star; the desire to entertain (see, for example, John Carpenter's *Fog* [1980], with its enunciated inscription of a storytelling function into the very text of the film in the figure of a storyteller); a joy in self-reflexive play; or, in a communication pure and simple by the material about itself, the filmmaker absented or reduced to an effect of the text. In the structural film, for example, the material of film becomes a kind of author: the film's sprocket holes or its dirt particles (as in George Landow's *Film in Which There Appear Sprocket Holes, Edge Lettering, Dirt Particles, etc.* [1965-66]) become its intentionality, its "I."

One of the primary aims, in fact, of the recent deconstructive readings of *Hollywood* films has been to suggest that it is in such works—precisely in texts from mass culture—that bourgeois ideology can be read in a critical way.[4] Indeed, any of the critical figurations of bourgeois ideology which Jameson finds in Wyndham Lewis; or which Eagleton finds in English literature from Austen to Conrad; or which MacCabe finds in Joyce, can be and have been found in any number of Hollywood films, and in the oeuvres of Hollywood directors from Douglas Sirk to Vincente Minnelli to Randall Keiser in his direction of *Grease*.[5] On the one hand, *Grease* seems to match perfectly the stereotypes that critics normally invoke to denigrate mass art: a simplicity of narrative line (boy meets girl, boy loses girl, boy gets girl); a reduction of visual complexity by a sharply coded iconography (the hero torn between blonde woman as incarnation of purity and the brunette as seething libido); an appeal to escapist fantasies (the fifties pictured without McCarthy, without Korea; youth gangs pictured as lovable and cute). On the other hand, it would be equally possible to find in *Grease* the very values that Jameson finds at work in Lewis. Jameson reads Lewis's work primarily as the figuration of agonistic relations which mediate the alienation and *agon* of life under capitalism. *Grease*, too, could be interpreted as an agonistic text; environments, as in Lewis, are not neutral backdrops in which actions proceed unhindered, but are virtual battlefields in which antagonistic characters can intrude at any moment, in which the threat of the Other is always present (the Rydell school principal steps into the hallway at the beginning of the film to break up a conversation between Danny Zucco and the members of his gang; another gang drives up to Rydell's pre-game bonfire to taunt Danny's gang; and so on), and in which the relation of characters to each other is a superficial one, without love, without real contact, and ultimately based on sham (Sandy must dress up as a "tough lady" at the end of the film to win Danny's affection, but one shot shows her discomfort in the role).

This is not to say that *Grease* is "moderately progressive to the extent that it manifests the terms of its own construction," as the Manchester Society for Education in Film and Television group suggests in its analysis of the film, but that it is possible to *read* the film and indeed any film, that way. This is to suggest that what is normally deemed the difference of the avant-garde is no difference at all, but a value that reading can establish anywhere. Indeed, if there is a singularity to the avant-garde project, this singularity is undoubtedly not some uniquely critical value but the persistence with which the avant-garde *proclaims* that critical value. The avant-garde is a genre among others, but, as

Eric de Kuyper suggests, it is the "mauvais genre," the genre that won't shut up ("Le mauvais genre," *CA* 18/19). The avant-garde is the art most committed to manifestos, to declarations, to polemics.[6] Significantly, its polemics take as their adversary not the economic and power relations of capitalist society itself but the (ostensible) representation of that society in mass culture. Mass culture, defined as an art that levels difference, becomes an equivalent to the processes of capitalism itself, and in this reduction, in this leveling act of its own, the avant-garde ethos can see itself as outside production, outside exchange, outside history.

One of the few Marxist attempts to deal with the social and economic position of avant-garde practice is the group of texts by Walter Benjamin, collected after his death as *Charles Baudelaire: A Lyric Poet in the Era of High Capitalism,* in which Benjamin tries to situate Baudelaire's practice—the seemingly rarified production of lyric poetry—in his era, a time in which lyric poetry is becoming irrelevant.[7] Benjamin presents the position of the modernist such as Baudelaire as an ambivalent one. On the one hand, Baudelaire wants to preserve the heroic status of the artist as a duplication of heroism in antiquity; but under capitalism, the only fate for heroism is for it to become a commodity: "Baudelaire knows what the true situation of the man of letters is: he goes to the marketplace as a *flâneur,* supposedly to take a look at it, but in reality to find a buyer" (p. 34). The avant-garde artist's position outside history is a position inside it; Benjamin's analysis is a metacommentary which starts from the seeming fact of the lyric poet's isolation in order to situate that isolation. The poet, like everyone, needs to survive, needs to enter the market, but the presence of that necessity can only be registered as a shock (a term which Benjamin intends quite specifically to refer to Freud's notion of physical shocks against which a consciousness must wield its defensive mechanisms); the transforming qualities of art serve as the artist's defense: "[Baudelaire] is on the lookout for banal incidents in order to approximate them to poetic events" (p. 99). The lyric poet does not merely write, but writes against. In an age characterized by "the disintegration of aura in the experience of shock," the poet finds that poetry becomes a combative, antagonistic, indeed agonistic, act:[8] "there is no daydreaming surrender to faraway things in the protective eye" (p. 151). What in a more gentle and utopian avant-garde expresses itself with seemingly innocent intent as the picturing of a pastoral world beyond contradiction (as, for example, in Connie Beeson's erotic tone-poem films of beautiful people making beautiful love on beautiful beaches and in beautiful woods) emerges in other avant-garde work in a savage attempt to deny, to wipe clear, the force of the status quo, the imposition of history. For example, Stan Brakhage's close-up filming of the scandalous sight of dead flesh in *Act of Seeing with One's Own Eyes,* or the stroboscopic and aural assault on the viewer's psycho-physiological responses in Paul Sharits's *T.O,U,C,H,I,N,G*

(1968) both demonstrate an insistence on the limitations of a certain kind of sight—a sight which it is the goal of the avant-garde film to aggress against. The works of the avant-garde may be *read* as so many options in the condition of artistic alienation: "to take inventory of the various possible symbolic reactions to this situation [of alienation] would involve an anatomy of modernism in all the ranges of its stylization, from efforts to transcend reason and logic, as hostages of a degraded culture or reality principle, all the way to the attempt to extirpate matter as such and to make language the space for some pure and liberated play of spirit beyond contingency" (Jameson, *Fables of Agression,* p. 39). In Baudelaire, as Benjamin reads him, the symbolic action is a denial through marginalization: Baudelaire looks at the city, the threatening world of his social *pratico-inert,* and transforms what is habitual or commonplace about the city into the eccentric and the exceptional—either the too high or the too low. Paris, as Baudelaire figures it, is not the city of the businessman, of the bourgeoisie, but of the drunkard, the ragpicker, the whore, on the one hand, and the hero, the dandy, the god, on the other; or the two together, the ragpicker become hero, the whore as goddess. But it is the commodity-world, the middle range of the everyday, that is the structuring absence for this transformative poetry.

Benjamin's reading of Baudelaire suggests that avant-garde activity is itself some kind of combat. Each of Baudelaire's forays into the crowded city becomes a kind of engagement with the enemy (remember, too, Breton's definition of the ultimate Surrealist act as the emptying of a loaded revolver into a crowd, or Ionesco's dream of machine-gunning the audience at the end of each performance of *The Bald Soprano*): "The shocks which his [Baudelaire's] worries caused him and the hundred ideas with which he *parried* them were reproduced by Baudelaire the poet in the *feints* of his prosody. To recognize the labour that Baudelaire bestowed upon his poems under the image of *fencing* means to learn to comprehend them as a continuous series of tiny improvisations. . . . In those days he had, symbolically speaking, set out to capture the streets" (p. 70, my emphasis). Style and stylus—the lyric poet uses his/her tools as so many means of denial, as weapons, as forms of a nonacceptance of a situation the inescapability of which is ultimately beyond the force of mere acceptance or not.

Where the lyric poet uses his/her stylus as a weapon in the combat of the streets, today's avant-garde artist straps on a sixteen-millimeter camera or a video-pack. This indeed is the subject of *David Holzmann's Diary* (Jim McBride, 1970): experiencing a loss of self, trying to find himself, a film buff straps on his camera and tries to turn the experiences of his New York world into film experiences so that he can gain a distance from his life and examine it. The film we see is the film he has shot: the awkward and uneven movement as he sneaks into a bedroom to film his girlfriend as she sleeps; his attempt to remain calm as a hooker confronts him and his sexuality; we even witness the filmmaker himself when he seats himself across from the camera for a face-on confession. Holzmann tries to mediate the shock of the world around him, to turn it into aesthetic form; in one scene, for example, he films the first and the last frame of every shot of television from sundown to sunrise to create a virtual inventory of the images of mass culture in which he is immersed, a survey not unlike the literary physiologies so rampant in Baudelaire's nineteenth century. Ultimately, the film presents its fullest defense: an end-title reveals that the film is scripted and that David Holzmann is played by an actor. The crush of experience, the encounter with the social other, receives an extreme mediation; it becomes a joke against that supreme other which the artist faces: the audience.

Before this unveiling, however, *David Holzmann's Diary* makes manifest one of the central paradoxes in a cinematic avant-garde: a desire to outrun the imputed alienation of the modern world, figured as a *technological* alienation, through technology—the equipment of a film—itself. As Benjamin presents Baudelaire, the lyric poet is on the edge of a technological revolution: "technology has subjected the human sensorium to a complete kind of training" (p. 132). Significantly, the crisis of situation that technology encourages shows up centrally in practices like photography, which make certain artistic practices irrelevant or consign them to the realm of the artisanal, and, furthermore, add to the very stockpile of mechanisms of shock: "of the countless movements of switching, inserting, pressing, and the like, the 'snapping' of the photographer has had the greatest consequences. A touch of the finger now sufficed to fix an event for an unlimited period of time" (p. 132). For Baudelaire, the tools of the poet still brought him/her back to a pretechnological artistic mode of production. For the experimental filmmaker, though, the presence of a supportive artisanal culture is no longer a given; it is a culture that if possible at all, has to be constructed.

Stan Brakhage, for example, would most seem to recreate a myth of the modernist as artisan. He stays within the conditions of cheap filmmaking—he is one of the few avant-gardists to have made a large portion of his films in eight millimeter, even though he owns sixteen-millimeter equipment—and tries consciously to live an artisanal life. For Brakhage, as for the *flâneur*, the city is the world one comes to stroll in and through (his real home is a cabin in Colorado) and to engage in furtive combat in and with (his verbal assaults on audiences are legion).

Brakhage's films seem to fall into three types, each of which reveals an experience of the modern, of the urban social. First, there are the personal-lyric films—the images of a party of friends in one of Brakhage's earliest films (*Desistfilm*, 1954), of his wife giving birth to their children (for example, *Window Water, Baby Moving*, 1959), of his lovemaking (*Wedlock House: an Intercourse*, 1959)—which recreate the security of an intimate space and try to find poetry in the personal (for example, the scenes of lovemaking in *Wedlock*

House are abstracted by negative footage). Second, there are the "transcendental" films—like the personal lyrics in form but not about personal events—in which the camera seeks to remove the concrete foundations—the situation—of objects and events. In Brakhage's *Anticipation of the Night* (1958), for example, the camera moves so quickly as to blur shapes in the backyard of a house, turning them into pure form; the least abstracted shots are of a faraway city late at night, shot from across a desert so that its reality becomes nothing more than a play of lights. The city is a thing to be held at a distance, transformed, aestheticized. This experience of the city as other, as danger, is confirmed in the third area of film in which Brakhage works: his city films, represented by the Pittsburgh trilogy—*eyes* (1970), *Deus ex* (1971), and *The Act of Seeing with One's Own Eyes* (1971). Here Brakhage confronts the city, slows his camera movement, and reduces his abstraction to reveal the perceived morbidity of everyday social life. In his discussion of the trilogy, P. Adam Sitney sees Brakhage's concern here as a defense against the "horrors of solipsism," the personalism of the other films: "in fact, several quasi-documentary films [the Pittsburgh trilogy] from this period . . . constitute attempts to ground his perception in a firmly established exterior reality (the police, a hospital, a morgue) as a brake to his excessive and frightening tendency to interiorize all that he sees" (*Visionary Cinema,* p. 421). Significantly, though, it is more the Pittsburgh trilogy that would appear to reveal a tendency toward the "excessive and frightening": this would be the horror that Brakhage sees as endemic to the world of the public.

In *Act of Seeing,* Brakhage significantly reverses the abstracting procedures of his solipsistic films; whereas in those films Brakhage renders abstract a world around him (for example, in *Text of Light,* made after the trilogy, Brakhage shoots the natural world through a crystal ashtray which becomes an extension of the film lens), here, in his presentation of autopsy procedures, he moves from abstraction to an increasing concretization. The opening shot is of a fuzzy, bright red, wrinkled mass—a virtually pure aesthetic image. But rather than remain in this world of the made-strange, rather than venture farther into that world, Brakhage focuses the image so that we can see it as a blanket covering a corpse. The film registers a brute world of brute facticity—the camera at one point shows a fly crawling against the background of some body part—and suggests that this facticity is stronger than any poesis. Indeed, the film's only options are a doomed poesis or a banality of horror. Poesis: after focusing on the swollen testicles of a corpse, the film suddenly goes blurry as if to transform the rot of death, but this aestheticizing attempt inevitably fails; the next shot returns to death, carefully documented, thrust back into clear image. Banal horror: the film poet disqualifies his powers as abstractor in the face of a different and more powerful and more painful kind of abstracting: the surgeons of the autopsy room turn human identity into pieces of flesh, they are the real transformers, the real poets. We see, for example, the procedures by which the surgeons remove the brain of a victim: they loosen skin around the scalp and literally pull the face down like a flap, which then folds up at the chin. This is the true abstracting process, an activity of change against which the abstracting qualities of poesis have only an inefficient and mock claim.

Significantly, Brakhage inserts the presence of his own self as fact into the film; specifically, we see the nervous jiggle of the camera as Brakhage is faced with particularly gruesome sights.[9] Here, more than in the lyric films, the filmmaker is in the presence of a world whose presentness cannot be denied or overlooked. Whereas the lyric films present a loss of the self through an attempted transcendence, the city films re-place that self in the everyday world where people can be torn apart in the cold anonymity of a white-walled room. The last shot of *Act of Seeing* shows a coroner dictating his report into a tape recorder. There is no end title; the film simply runs out on this image of a city worker. This authority, this man who is more a poet of death than the lyric artist, is the truth of the city, its significance. The city films form an interruption in Brakhage's career; they can stand as a document of that which the other films work to repress. The camera itself, that eye which can register the city in all its hereness, must itself be transformed in the non-city films—ashtrays must be put over the lens, film with sensitivity to special colors must be used, negative footage must be introduced.

Brakhage's work is an extreme version of the city/country split which so underlies the experience of art, including avant-garde art, in the age of high capitalism. Indeed, it is possible to construct a typology of the avant-garde in terms of the stances the films take (consciously or not) toward social experience. Such a typology would bring into question the kind of typology of avant-garde cinema that P. Adam Sitney provides in his *Visionary Camera: The American Avant-Garde Film, 1943-1978*, one that has informed much investigation of American experimental film. The point would be to suggest not that Sitney's typology is useless (although one could well raise questions, for example, about the films he includes, the theoretical framework he uses to discuss those films, and the ends to which he intends his typology to be used),[10] but rather that it is incomplete, lacking the kind of metacommentary that could concretize its categories in history.

Sitney suggests that American avant-garde film is best read through concepts of Romantic poetics ("I have found this approach consistently more useful and more generative of a unified view of these films and filmmakers than the Freudian hermeneutics and sexual analyses which have dominated much of the previous criticism of the American avant-garde film"—p. x) and he isolates five major strands in American avant-garde film, seeing each strand as dominant in a particular moment of the American avant-garde cinema's history. The trance film, exemplified in the films of Maya Deren, chronicles an interior quest in which a hero or a heroine "encounters objects and sights as if they were capable of revealing the erotic mystery of the self" (p. 11). The lyrical film, exemplified for Sitney by Brakhage, puts the hero or heroine behind the camera, situating the process of discovery in the movements and discoveries of the camera itself; it is a kind of literal shift into first-person. They mythopoeic film expands this quest, "with a corresponding shift from Freudian preoccupations to those of Jung" (p. 31), into an investigation of broad symbolic structures, an investigation which may or may not find a localization in the figure of a hero or heroine. In the structural film, the apparatus of film engages in an investigation of its own selfness; meaning is not out "there" in either the filmmaker's psyche or in transcendental archetypes, but in the fact of film itself: "the structural film approaches the conditions of meditation and evokes states of consciousness without mediation; that is, with the sole mediation of the camera" (p. 370). The participatory film, an offshoot of structural film, removes the quest from the process internal to a film and creates a quest between spectator and cinema, for example, George Landow's *Institutional Quality* (1969), which parodies training films, or Robert Nelson's *Blue Shirt* (1970), in which spectators play along with attempts to guess the right name of various boats.

Lacking any attention to history, other than a kind of internal history in which films automatically align themselves into traditions, Sitney's approach can only classify films and not explain them—except in terms of the categories themselves. Sitney is right to note that there are subgenres in the genre of American experimental film, but without a conception of history he is unable to explain anything about the significance of these subgenres, and for most of the book he engages in mere and extended description of the films. There is an untheorized appeal to influence (Sitney opens the first chapter with the declaration that the work of Maya Deren and Alexander Hammid "recalls" the collaboration of Luis Bunuel and Salvador Dali in *Un chien andalou* but later mentions that "it is possible that neither Hammid nor Deren had seen the Dali-Bunuel film before they made theirs"—p. 15), and to a logic of the typology, to a sense that the categories each naturally generate the next category according to a teleological and organic necessity. But such a philosophy of causation finds itself continually challenged by the irreducibility of the historical event to its theoretical explanation. For example, in discussing the rise of structural film and the interest of a number of already established filmmakers in this new subgenre, Sitney admits that "just why, at approximately the same time, Stan Brakhage, Gregory Markopoulos, Bruce Baillie, and Ken Jacobs began to extend their work in this direction is difficult to determine" (p. 174). This difficulty seems to be a consequence of Sitney's inability to understand tradition as anything but the influence of one filmmaker on another (Sitney acknowledges the strong influence of Harold Bloom on his work); typically, Sitney answers the question of this difficulty with the suggestion that "Warhol's

sudden shock blow to the aesthetics of the avant-garde film was a factor...,"
but why this was registered as a shock blow, what other factors might have been
significant, are questions Sitney does not address. Instead, he jumps
immediately from his suggestion about Warhol to a description of structural
films, as if the question of their "origin" had now been laid peacefully to rest.

A typology of the avant-garde film would not necessarily reject Sitney's
categories, but would explain them. For example, Lucien Goldmann's
analysis, in *Pour une sociologie du roman* (1964), of the loss of the human
subject in novels like those of Robbe-Grillet in relation to the loss of the subject
under monopoly capitalism might well be used to explain a similar process in
the structural film. Indeed, the structural filmmakers rely on the theoretical
suppositions of structuralism and its reflection in the literary practice of the
New Novel. The structural film works to banish emotion, identification, and
intrigue from art in order to eliminate qualities that the filmmakers view as
foreign to the work itself; there is in such an ideology of artistic purity,
supposedly achieved through such paring down of material, a kind of
technologism, a faith that technology will save us from the all-too-human. In
this, the structural project carries on a critique of humanism but one which can
fit well with an ideology of bourgeois rationality and productivity.[11]

In an establishing film of the American avant-grade, Deren and Hammid's
Meshes of the Afternoon, the social tensions of the quest, of the trance film as
Sitney describes it, are already present. Commonly seen as a retreat into
interiority, *Meshes* is more about the doomed battle of interiority *against*
forces from outside. In it a woman (played by Deren) alone in a house
confronts objects around her—a flower, a telephone, a knife, and, most
horrifyingly, duplicates of her own self—in a kind of agonistic relationship, as
so many symbols laden not only with meaning, but with threat. Into this
psychodrama, a man, dressed in normal clothes (the woman is dressed
exotically in a long, flowing pants outfit, and has billowing, wavy hair), enters
to establish the normalcy of those objects seen to be menacing (the telephone is
just a telephone; the duplicate women are mere phantasms), but seems to be
killed by the woman as he begins to caress her body. With a jarring cut, we see
the man once more enter the house to find the woman dead, her throat cut.
Sitney compares *Meshes* to Bunuel's and Dali's *Un chien andalou,* but such a
comparison can obscure the narrative line of *Meshes,* which is not fully the ode
to unreason that the Dali-Bunuel film represents. In *Un chien andalou,* Dali
and Bunuel rigorously reject any postition that would ground the strange
events in a particular consciousness; if the film is fantastic, it is so for the
spectator but not for the characters, who are themselves part of the fantastic
structure. Ultimately, *Un chien andalou* asserts a decidability in the form of
allegory, its reality lies in its suggestions about repetition, about the ties
between desire and violence, about forms of authority. For all its unreason, the
film is no less about the social; indeed, the Surrealist dissociation of objects

takes place against the backdrop of a concretely pictured Paris. It is in that Paris that logic gives way. In contrast, the social world in *Meshes* is not a backdrop, but the very world in which the character of Deren acts out her agon. The objects that Deren confronts are not the ants pouring out of a hand or the rotting donkeys atop pianos of *Un chien andalou,* but everyday objects that are endowed with meaning. *Meshes* localizes the view of the fantastic in one person; when the man appears, the fantastic, figured in phallic objects, can reveal itself to be the projection of the woman's sexual fears. If *Meshes of the Afternoon* is to be compared to any earlier experimental film, the appropriate choice would more likely be something like *Cabinet of Dr. Caligari* (Wiene, 1919) which uses a similar *mise-en-abime* structure to localize *folie* in a particular consciousness. *Meshes* is expression rather than surrealist and shares *Caligari*'s attempt to shift from the expressionist of a single consciousness to an outsider's view of that consciousness. Moreover, like *Caligari, Meshes* complicates this escape from the interiority of a singular point of view. *Caligari*'s framing story, in which we see the hero in an insane asylum, is shot in the same expressionist style as the scenes which denote the hero's story proper; the final scene of *Meshes* shows the woman dead, killed somehow by fantasies, though previous scenes had tried to discredit the objective status of those fantasies.

Meshes can represent the filmic impossibility of the lyric tradition that Benjamin describes in *Charles Baudelaire;* like the nineteenth-century lyric, the film figures alienation and petit-bourgeois despair as the threat of the social, the quotidian world pictured as so many potential shocks. But unlike lyric poetry, which grasps the fact that it is still a pretechnological form of production, *Meshes* presents the very tools of the modern poetic or cinematic act as part of that shock. The camera technique, the disjunctive editing especially, is part of the threat; the camera techniques become a kind of objective, external force manipulating the heroine (for example, as she tries to climb a set of stairs, the movement of the camera buffets her back and forth), producing her doubles (through trick photography), and making objects from the world all the more threatening (for example, the knife, which one of her doubles will use to attack her, is shown in extreme close-up, the shiny metal creating a distorted reflection of the heroine's face). Benjamin suggests that in Baudelaire there is a concern with "inorganic things which was one of his sources of inspiration...the [second "Spleen"] poem is entirely based on empathy with material that is dead in a dual sense. It is inorganic matter that has been eliminated from the circulation process" (pp. 55-56). Baudelaire's lyric poetry is a backward glance, an attempt to animate dead objects, to restore aura ("the murmur of the past may be heard in the correspondences"—p. 141). But in *Meshes,* no backward glance is possible; here are not eccentric objects with no practical function, but practical forces with a vitality and a direct tie to the everyday world (from an ordinary kitchen knife or a front door key to an average-looking man to the apparatus of the cinema itself). In a sense, this is merely the extension of the situation Benjamin attributes to Baudelaire. Baudelaire's situation as poet is one in which he himself has been objectified, turned into a commodity, and the backward glance, the spiritual communion with noncommodities is a way of fundamentally denying the omnipresence of the commodity: "the *flâneur* is someone abandoned in the crowd. In this, he shares the situation of the commodity. He is not aware of this special situation, but it permeates him blissfully like a narcotic that can compensate him for many humiliations" (p. 55). In *Meshes,* the recognition that everything, including one's self, can be objectified, comes forth in all its intensity; the film is a kind of negative lyric in which the possibility for allegory, for transforming a situation, is finally closed. In this situation, death can seem an inevitability. "The resistance which modernism offers to the natural productive élan of a person is out of proportion to his strength. It is understandable if a person grows tired and takes refuge in death. Modernism must be under the sign of a suicide, an act which seals a heroic will that makes no concessions to a mentality inimical towards this will" (Benjamin, p. 75).

Between heroic death and the *flâneur's* lyric and allegorical stance—a stance that leaves an artist like Baudelaire powerless—Benjamin outlines a number of other options for artistic production under capitalism. Benjamin tends to see these options as embracing the commodity system, and he points out their financial success in great detail, But it is equally possible to see such options taken up by the avant-garde, too, as ways of admitting the presence of the social but trying to dampen its force. The first of these options is the physiological sketch; the sketch is a catalogue of objects, events, figures in the world, but with an emphasis on the exceptional examples, on the cases that stand outside the ordinary, (hopefully) outside the commodity. "These writings were socially dubious, too. The long series of eccentric or simple, attractive or severe figures which the physiologies presented to the public in character sketches had one thing in common: they were harmless and of perfect bonhomie. Such a view of one's fellow man was so remote from experience that there were bound to be uncommonly weighty motives for it. The reason was an uneasiness of a special sort" (p. 37).

With its ideology of difference, the avant-garde finds in the physiology a perfect form in which it can register difference.[12] An early example of a physiologic film in the American avant-garde is Frank Stauffacher's *Sausalito* (1948), which hovers between lyric and documentary film in its poetic montage of images of Sausalito. What the film emphasizes is Sausalito's apartness—this is not a town like any other, but a special place. At the same time, though, one can see elements, kept to a minimum, here, that will emerge in full force in another genre—the film of menace and *angst.* A few shots in *Sausalito,* such as that of an eye looking through a hole in a fence or of a pair of feet fleeing from the frame, add a sense of menace to the innocence of the physiology.[13]

The film physiology is like the lyric text in its desire to disguise the problems of the everyday world; indeed, the two genres come together in a film like *Castro Street* (Bruce Baillie, 1966), which catalogues the events along an industrial street but also transforms those events through various forms of trick photography. The physiology moves toward a comic register by a virtual fetishizing of seemingly irrelevant or uncommon sights. For much of its running length, *O Dem Watermelons* (Robert Nelson, 1963-65) is a comic physiology which pretends that the fate of watermelons is of extreme importance. The first shot, after the credits, is of a watermelon lying in the grass; the shot holds for at least a minute when the melon suddenly turns into a football kicked into the air. The film then proceeds to catalogue a number of events involving watermelons: they are shot; they are stepped on; they are cut by swords; they are chopped open by a butcher; they are made love to by a woman. The spectatorial pleasure of such incidents seems to derive from their unseriousness, indeed their total absurdity. However, Nelson is using the physiology form to criticize the very innocence of a physiological approach to everyday life, the way the physiology (and the spectator) catalogues supposed differences in the world. Through juxtapositions which get stronger as the film progresses, the watermelons become associated with blacks. The film thus works first to encourage a seemingly innocent spectatorial pleasure—starting out as an eccentric oddity—but then progressively politicizes this innocence, qualifies it.

Benjamin suggests a central problem with the physiologies; namely, that their innocence will constantly be belied by social reality: "... the physiologies helped fashion the phantasmagoria of Paris life in their own way. But their methods could not get them very far. People knew one another as debtors and creditors, salesmen and customers, employers and employees, and above all as competitors. In the long run, it did not seem very likely that they could be made to believe that their associates were harmless oddballs" (p. 39). Although they are not about oddballs but about beautiful people (oddballs of a different sort), Connie Beeson's films—for example, *Thenow* (1970), *Holding* (1971)—suffer for many people precisely because the exceptional world they present—perfect beaches (with no crowds) with perfect-shaped (and usually Caucasian) people gambling and making love—is in complete disparity to a world which is anything but perfect or beautiful. Benjamin suggests that a solution for the physiologies was to move toward a more engaged and aggressive stance toward the social world; the physiologies became empirical, suggesting that a careful cataloguing of the ordinary, rather than the eccentric world, was now the order of the day and might lead to a taming of that world. "They assured people that everyone was, unencumbered by any factual knowledge, able to make out the profession, the character, the background, and the life-style of passers-by. . . . If that sort of thing could be done, then, to be sure, life in the big city was not nearly so disquieting as it probably seemed to people" (p. 39). The empirical physiology catalogues not the phantasmagoria of the city but its ordinariness, and it aspires to confidence simply by the fact that ordinariness can indeed be catalogued. Certain of Bruce Conner's films—films which generally use found footage and no newly shot material—reveal a pop art sensibility and a concern to turn the images of social life into clichés simply through the impassive stare of the camera. In *Crossroads* (1968), for example, Conner edits together thirty minutes of official military footage of the Bikini Atoll A-Bomb test to render that image ultimately banal. Conner doesn't alter the footage but simply allows the explosion to present and re-present itself in all its directness until we can understand it, can have a hold over it. Similar to this is Conner's film of another bombshell, Marilyn Monroe: *Marilyn x 5* (1973), which loop-prints an image of a strip-teasing woman (who may or may not be Marilyn Monroe) so that we see the same scene five times, set to a similarly repeated soundtrack of Monroe singing "I'm through with love." Again, a pop image of American life loses its force (in many of his films Conner pictures women as simply a reserve of dangerous, virtually libidinal energy needing containment) and becomes ordinary, quotidian in the dullest sense.

Chantal Ackerman, in her New York film *News From Home* (1976), reveals a sensibility toward New York City that is similar to pop art's "empirical" cataloguing of everyday sights in America. For most of *News From Home*, a ninety-minute film, the camera stares impassively at streets of New York. Each shot lasts for at least several minutes with no camera action. There is a certain lyrical side to the film; the film stock accentuates reds and greens so that the first shot, for example, down a long city street on the lower West Side, achieves a kind of formal(ist) beauty from the way brake lights suddenly illumine in a burst of red as cars reach what must obviously be a stop-sign far in the background of the frame.[14] But, for the most part, the film registers the facticity of the city—for example, a man sitting in the night under the fluorescent green lights of a gas station—and banishes lyricism through distancing techniques such as the very uneventful *durée* of each shot. The city seems not to be judged; it is simply there, an inert form. Ackerman goes on, though, to qualify this inertness, to call the myth of empiricism into question. One never simply sees an object, but instead filters it through conceptual frameworks. *News From Home* reasserts the city as a (negative) value by introducing two foreign elements, two variants, into the formal structure its stasis has established. First, after an initial silence, a voice intrudes every so often on the soundtrack—the voice of Ackerman's mother in Brussels—telling of news from home (Ackerman is Belgian by birth) and worrying about her daughter's life in America and the big city. The mother is a fount of traditional values, and against that tradition, Ackerman must build her own space, in the only space available to her—the space of the city. But since the city is inert, a brute Other, Ackerman resorts to the only option she has, short of lyrical idealism, to manipulate that space, assert a control over it: in the second kind of variation on the initial premises of the film, Ackerman introduces camera movement about halfway into the film. After ten or so long shots with no movement, the camera suddenly begins to pivot, attempting to discover a freedom of expression, a voice. But the movement is an ambiguous one: a smooth, geometric, 360-degree pan that ends up where it started from. Ackerman's camera seems caught between the liberatory gesture of altering the empirical through cinematic means and the final realization that this engagement on the level of technique changes nothing about that empirical reality. (There is never, for example, any recognition by people in the frame that they are being filmed.) Indeed, empirical reality seems to reemerge in full force at the end of the film. The last shot, from the back of a boat, moves with great fluidity as the boat curves its way out from the port of New York; the mother's voice on the soundtrack makes it clear that Ackerman is returning home, to the world of family. Movement, the powers of technique, are no guarantee of escape from the empirical, from tradition, from the impositions of a kind of history. By engaging in a meditation on the form, *News From Home* pinpoints some of the values at stake in empirical physiology.

In its concern with long-held shots that will then enter into a strict binary opposition with camera movement later on in the film, *News From Home* shares some of the interest of that extreme form of cataloguing film, the structural film. The structural film is both the logical culmination of the physiology, and its negation. Filtering out everything in the film experience that is inert, that is simply an observable fact, the structural film engages in an ostensible purification to try to push the field of the Other outside the film and to give the filmmaker full control of what happens in the film. There is an attempt to turn the film into pure bits of an artificial language, with any referent reduced to a minimum. In George Landow's *Film in Which There Appear Sprocket Holes, Edge Lettering, Dirt Particles, etc.*, the only pre-filmic event is another film—a piece of test footage of a girl blinking (whether once or not is not determinable; Landow loop-prints the "action" to make it mechanical) over which there is another subject—the sprocket holes, the scratches, etc., which play across the image of the woman for the five-minute duration of the film. Writing about structural film, Peter Wollen notes how the supposed materialism of such a cinema is actually a repetition of the *ontological* investigations of Bazin and realist theorists ("Ontology and Materialism in Film," *Screen,* 1976). While rejecting Bazin's valorization of an ontology of the *photographic* image as an indexical registering of an extra-filmic reality, the structural avant-garde merely inverts terms, and never really breaks from a belief that there is a nature of film. Structural theory continues to see an ontology of film, as Bazin did, but displaces this ontology from what is in the image to the fact of the image, its "material substrata," in Wollen's terms. For Landow, for example, film is essentially nothing but sprocket holes, edge lettering, etc., and everything else—character, story, drama—are so many foreign elements. Landow's solution is to try to bring the material of the film to the surface, into prominence. This procedure, however, has the air of a defensive gesture; the outside, the social, is viewed as so much contingent, virtually menacing, matter, and the filmmaker must become a scientist working on formal combinations in the safety of a laboratory. In Peter Gidal's writing about his own structural film practice, there is an ever-increasing elimination of elements deemed to be reactionary: not merely the commercial film, but modernist films of ambiguity: "ambiguousness aligns itself as a concept (and therefore as a reality) with the concept of freedom and individualism.... Our whole formation towards, and in, filmic enterprises, is dominated by such ideological strangleholds" (introduction to *Structural Film Anthology*, p. 4). Deconstructive manipulation of codes of film is also found to be ultimately no more than an endorsement of the codes: "Deconstruction exercises, maintained filmically (i.e., on film in film) are direct translations from the written into film and are thus filmically reactionary..." (p. 5). In such a retreat into the supposed surety of film material and form, the structural film reveals its attitude toward the social, indeed its fear of that social.

A very different approach is one that admits the presence of the social but views it as some kind of phantasmic force, not really social after all. With its camera movement, *News From Home* breaks from the structural problem to render its earlier view of the city—as a merely neutral force—invalid. The city is not simply there, but it is there as a burden, a force to be reckoned with. In this retrospection, which challenges the escapist laboratory purity of formal experimentation, *News From Home* takes on a social form not unlike the third form of literature which Benjamin sees as permeating the nineteenth century: an art of malaise, art about the disquieting, malevolent aspects of the social. "The soothing little remedies which the physiologists offered for sale were soon passé. On the other hand, the literature which concerned itself with the disquieting and threatening aspects of urban life was to have a greater future" (p. 40). Unlike the lyric, such art sees social reality as too powerful to be merely aestheticized. At the same time, such a social reality is not a reality *out there*, a physiology, and so, susceptible to a safe cataloguing; it is a force that is encroaching on the individual, an active power of alienation. At its extreme, this registering of the force of the social can expand into the despair of rage, the spleen that many critics have seen as the underlying dynamic of avant-garde aesthetics.

Significantly, though, when the avant-garde artist tries to give figuration to what he/she reads as metaphysical alienation, the figures arrived at are easily readable as displacements of social fears, and not metaphysical ones. In many of the films of male filmmakers, for example, the symbol of threat is figured as female, a displacement of the specific social concerns of patriarchy into a form which aspires to the universal and mythological. In this mythology—the reverse of Baudelaire's elevation of the prostitute into a goddess—the woman is the source of loss, of destruction of (male) selfhood. In Kenneth Anger's *Rabbit's Moon* (1969) and Bruce Conner's *Cosmic Ray* (1961), the filmmakers set up a lyric situation that the intrusion of woman as threat, as literal femme fatale, undermines. The lyric relationship is a specular one: the viewer (in the film or watching the film) *views* the objects of experience in an attempt at transcendence. In the lyric experience, that which we look at "reflects back at us that of which our eyes will never have their fill . . . the essentially distant is the inapproachable; inapproachability is in fact a primary quality of the ceremonial image" (Benjamin, pp. 146-48). In the lyric, the woman maintains a distance; either the woman stays where she is, as in Conner's *Vivian* (1966) which has the woman dancing as pure spectacle through the rooms of a museum to the fetishizing music of Nat King Cole singing "Mona Lisa," or, if the distance is broken, this occurs as a decision on the part of the observer, and not the woman—as in Standish Lawder's *Corridor* (1970) in which long tracking shots down a corridor finally encounter a nude woman at the end, signifier of sense, the meaning of the camera's epistemological voyage.

In *Rabbit's Moon* and *Cosmic Ray*, the filmmakers reveal a fear of what happens if the boundaries of the specular relationship are broken, if lyric specularity is destroyed through what Jeffrey Mehlman refers to as the "irruption of a third element which in its heterogeneity, asymmetry and unexpectedness, breaks the unity of two specular terms and rots away their closure" (*Revolution and Repetition*, p. 14). Both films begin with the seeming innocence and idealism of the lyric. In *Rabbit's Moon*, a Pierrot figure prays to the moon from a setting turned a pale blue by the film stock Anger is using. In *Cosmic Ray*, Conner tries to imagine the inner vision of blind singer Ray Charles through kinetic images of exuberance and plenitude (a woman dancing, fireworks, scintillating lights). In both films, the hero is on a quest for meaning, and a woman appears as promise of that meaning—a fairy queen in Anger's film, the dancing woman with her joie-de-vivre in Conner's. But, in both cases, the woman turns out to be a threat. In *Rabbit's Moon* she tempts Pierrot only to abandon him for another and leave him dead among the fallen leaves. In *Cosmic Ray* the woman herself becomes an explicit force of loss and death; halfway through the film, she begins to sport a skull over her genital region, and Conner intercuts her dance with images (from an old Mickey Mouse cartoon) of phallic cannon firing and then wilting as the woman's dance becomes more frenetic. Both films are mock lyrics, recognizing the impossibility of transcending an existence that is altogether too earthbound. In Anger's film, in particular, the farcical impossibility of transcendence is underscored by a soundtrack composed of nothing but American fifties golden oldies (for example, "I Only Have Eyes for You"), which reinvest a world of pop iconography into the film to deflate its magical setting.

It might seem that this subgenre—the texts which recognize worldly horror— possesses a socially critical edge that is lacking in the more pastoral aspirations of the lyric. This, for example, is Jameson's argument for the revolutionary potential of Wyndham Lewis: "the most authentic realization of the ancient epic ideal in modern times yields not some decorative and beautiful pastiches, but rather the most jarring and energetic mimesis of the mechanical, and breathes a passionate revulsion for that great automobile graveyard which is the 'modern mind'" (*Fables*, p. 80). But the very energy Jameson professes to find in Lewis attests to a kind of *distorting* power in social-horror art that is no less a transformation, a containment, of the social than the lyric or the structural or the physiological. The very fact that the art of, say, Lewis or of Anger or of Conner registers the social world as horror, as a virtually evil force, a veritable agon of self and environment, suggests a kind of exaggeration, an elementary reification in which social relations are turned into virtually metaphysical relations (the Other as evil incarnate) or relations between a person and objects of experience. (See, for example, the anthropomorphism of rooms which Jameson shows to be at work in Lewis's novels.) In Paul Bartel's *Secret Cinema* (1966), for example, the heroine, Joan, finds that her whole environment is a threatening one; wherever she goes, Joan has the feeling that she is being filmed, an impression that is confirmed when she enters a movie theater only to find that the film playing is her life, *The Story of Joan*. As Joan goes from friend to friend looking for solace, only to find that each friend has his or her secret camera, the city itself becomes part of Joan's oppression, the dark shadows descending around her, virtually engulfing her, increasing her alienation. This is a fetishizing of the social, no less mythic than, say, the cataloguing fetish in the physiology. Indeed, the very desire to understand the encounter of self and the social as an agon, however intensely that encounter is registered, is a mythic desire, in which the Other takes on the qualities of "the hyperbolic image" that Poggioli sees as the underlying poetic form of an agonistic avant-garde (*Theory of the Avant-Garde*, pp. 182-83). The very act of transforming the impositions of reality through hyperbole allows any defeat, any loss, in contact with that reality to be recorded as a heroic sacrifice: "The agonistic attitude is not a passive state of mind, exclusively dominated by a sense of imminent catastrophe; on the contrary, it strives to transform the catastrophe into a miracle. By acting, and through its very failure, it tends toward a result justifying and transcending itself . . . nothing better demonstrates the presence of an agonistic mentality in the avant-garde aesthetic consciousness than the frequency in modern poetry of what we shall call the hyperbolic image" (p. 66).

Most typologies of artistic practice, including the typology I've offered here, find themselves exceeded in some way by the diversity of that practice. Indeed, the interest of certain works of the avant-garde for many critics resides precisely in the ways those works seem to violate any typologizing, or, conversely, in the ways those works have seemed to suffer a reduction when dealt with inside the categories of a typology. Michael Snow's *Wavelength* (1967), for example, has held a special importance for theorists of the avant-garde because of its openness, the way it articulates a number of questions about avant-garde practice (which is not to say anything about its being a better or more politically important film).

The structure of *Wavelength* is deceptively simple: a camera zooms across a New York City loft from one end to the other for forty-three minutes—an action that is interrupted by several nonfilmic events (two women enter and listen to a radio; a man breaks in and seems to die on the floor) and several filmic ones (filter changes, film stock changes, several superimposed flashbacks and flashforwards). Many writers on the film have tried to categorize it through one set formula. Sitney, for example, classifies it as a film about cinematic structure, but subsequently violates his own categorizing by admitting that "the convergence of the two kinds of happening [filmic and nonfilmic] and their subsequent metamorphosis create for the viewer a continually changing experience of cinematic illusion and anti-illusion" (*Visionary Film,* p. 378).

In fact, *Wavelength* crosses categories and can be read to play off the kinds of categories used here to examine avant-garde films. There is, for example, a certain lyric quality to the film; it registers the starkness of the room and then offers a kind of transcendence through the purity of its zoom and that zoom's destination in a lyrical image—a photo of waves. But the film doesn't allow the lyric transcendence to come to fruition; there is an all-too-present everyday world which continually reveals the impossibility of the transcendent experience. On the one hand, the photo of the waves is, after all, a photo—it is not waves, but a mere simulacrum, pinned to the wall, contained in the room. More than that, as photo, it presents a flatness that is thereby an inadequate allegory of escape after the motion-in-depth of the camera; as if to emphasize the extent to which a flat image can only offer an empty lyricism, the film superimposes moments of the zoom onto the waves to present a depth that is not at all in the waves but only in the cinematic presentation of them. On the other hand, the ostensibly lyric path of the camera, its virtual determination, is interrupted by intrusions of the worldly: for example, the man who seems to die and thus initiates a hermeneutic coding (Who is the man? What has happened to him?) that plays against the forward move of the camera. The death, if that is indeed what it is, remains unsolved because the inexorable movement of the camera toward its goal slowly removes the man's body from presence in the frame. The hermeneutic concern is mechanically eliminated from the film by a film technique, a zoom, but that concern remains in viewer interest and is indeed revived when a woman later enters the room and telephones someone named Richard to tell him that there is a body on the floor.

Wavelength sets up at least two times—a lyric time and a hermeneutic time—and then juxtaposes this structure against other orders. As it asks its transcendental questions—for example, can the purity of a zoom lead to a trancelike state in the viewer?—the film also raises physiological questions: what does this room look like? What are those things on the far wall? All these questions are played out against a backdrop—the city street that we can see through a window just to the left of the waves photo and which disappears as the zoom reaches its end. For most of the film, this world outside could well seem to be the target of the zoom, the camera moving beyond the confinements of a room to a vibrant outside. But the course of the trajectory is to banish this outside which can then only return in figures, in the people whose entrances are first announced by noise (doors opening or, in the case of the man, glass breaking) and then by their visual presence. On the one hand, these human events have only a physiological value; their status as events becomes equivalent to filmic events—the sudden changes of stock or filter, for example; that is, in the sense of the Russian formalists, they are *devices* like any other.

Snow's answer to Simon Hartog's question, "Why does life enter the film?," suggests this sense of people as so many elements to be converted into components of a physiology that looks upon all its components with the same neutrality: "Life is in the film. One of the subjects of the film or perhaps more accurately what the film *is* is a balancing of different orders, classes of events and protagonists. The image of the yellow chair has as much 'value' in its own world as the girl closing the window" ("Ten Questions to Michael Snow," *Structural Film Anthology,* p. 36). But it is equally possible to read the presence of the human event as exceeding the cataloguing and formalizing surety of the physiology; like the art of malaise, of everyday horror, *Wavelength* registers the alienating experience of the environment, invoking the environment not as a neutral zone but as a value. Most explicitly invoking a kind of social menace is the figure of the man—the room is a room of crime (he enters illegally) and death. Critic Manny Farber, who has probably done the most to focus critical attention on a (virtually sociological) recognition of the poetics of the horror of everyday life in the American B-movie action film, captures some of the sense of the criminality in *Wavelength* by applying the values of the action film to it: "a pure, tough forty-five minutes that may become *The Birth of a Nation* in Underground Films...a straightforward document of a room in which a dozen businesses have lived and gone bankrupt" (*"Wavelength," Negative Space,* p. 250). As Farber reads it, *Wavelength* is virtually the deep structure of the action film: an inexorable move to a destined end, punctuated by a few high-pitch events.

This is to suggest that *Wavelength* is not only a film but one which makes explicit some of the elements in a theory of film. While this is, in a sense, true of every film—the fundamental structuring absence of every film is the metacommentary, the theory, which explains its project, situates it— *Wavelength* provides, as it were, more of the raw material that a metacommentary starts from (but it is not necessarily that metacommentary itself). Whereas a lyric film like Beeson's *Thenow* merely tries to figure a utopian space, *Wavelength* judges utopia against another space—here, specifically the room in its brute presence. Whereas a structural film like Landow's *Film in Which . . .* represses human action so that nothing but a repetitive eye-blinking remains, *Wavelength* interrupts its structural form with a variety of events and so figures a return of that repressed which the structural film is in retreat from. This is not to say that *Wavelenth* is more valuable than these other films. I am simply suggesting that, more than other experimental films, it makes explicit a set of values that are present in all films—the values of being in some way connected to human concerns, of being themselves a human concern, of reiterating the impossibility of more than relative autonomy, of always allowing a metacommentary that will establish the invincible connections of art to experience even when it tries to deny those connections at all costs.

4

The Politics of a Brechtian Aesthetics

> In reality, the critical attitude is the only productive one, the only one worthy of a person. It signifies collaboration, continuation, and life. Without a critical attitude, true artistic pleasure is impossible.
>
> Bertolt Brecht, "The Critical Attitude"

A reader coming (as I did) to Brecht's critical writings only after encountering the use made of Brecht in recent critical theory of art may well experience a kind of alienation-effect, a disparity between the current interpretation of Brecht, and what his words can seem to be saying.[1] Many current readings of Brecht employ a formalizing interpretation whereby one perspective—for example, his emphasis on a separation of elements—of Brecht's theory is extracted from the whole, and then peremptorily declared to be the whole of what Brecht was saying.[2] For example, in *James Joyce and the Revolution of the Word* (1979), Colin MacCabe reads the Brechtian aesthetic as one concerned essentially with rejecting traditional forms, in support of his claim that "Joyce's writing produces a change in the relations between reader and text, a change which has profound revolutionary implications" (p. 1). This version of Brecht is invoked continuously throughout MacCabe's book; Joyce's refusal to make reading easy is likened by MacCabe to Brecht's estrangement of the audience, and his defense of non-Aristotelean epic theatre: "[In Joyce,] deprived of a unitary position of dominance, the reader's discourses distance themselves one from the other as they declare their contradictions. The distances thus opened up provide the space for new things to be said. These methods of subverting the reading subject suggest that Joyce's texts can be considered as the novelistic equivalent of a Brechtian drama" (pp. 102-3). Brecht's concerns with popularity (not in the sense of success necessarily, but rather that of relevance), with realism, and, most importantly, with the subordination of any formal technique to a social technique—of a formal estrangement to an estrangement in and of the social—disappear as MacCabe constructs the Brecht he needs for his argument.[3]

In this, MacCabe's book is typical of a certain use in criticism,[4] a utilization that is directly connected to the schools and approaches criticized in previous chapters as potentially blocking an engagement with the complexity of a text's situation in the social. The formalist takeover of Brecht is a culmination of the formalist project. Understanding their adversary as the monolith of representation and narrative, formalist approaches have simply argued for an art that would reject or "subvert" these characteristics. Narrative and illusionism are seen by such theory to work together to banish, or suture, contradiction.

Illusionism, for example, supposedly does this by putting the spectator in fictive contact with a world reflected in the work of art, thereby hiding the work of the artistic text as a mediating force. Illusionism depends upon a conception of the subject-object duality as automatically—or, at the very least, inevitably—bridgeable in an act of passive contemplation or observation.[5] The world manifests, presents, truth and all one must do is contemplate that world—or its embodiment in those transparent conveyors that are works of art—to gain insight into that meaning.

The ideas of André Bazin clearly epitomize the application to film of this optimistic theory of the possibilities of meaning; indeed, new theories often begin with what is perceived to be a necessary critique of the imputed dominance of the Bazinian aesthetic. With such notions as the close-up as window to the soul, as the destructiveness of conscious artistic intervention, and of film as the revelation of the *vie intérieure* of the world, Bazin becomes the target for many, if not most, newer theories which see film as a production of meaning, as a site of work in the viewer's consciousness.

The problem with the critique of illusionism is not that illusionism doesn't exist; indeed, a requisite for any developing theory of film, including a political one, is the need to grapple with the virtually mythic dominance of the Bazinian aesthetic in thinking about film.[6] What polarizes the opposition to Bazin, prompting it to adopt an either/or position, with no room for other approaches, is the peremptory quality of Bazin's own approach, its claim to an understanding of the "ontology" of film, a claim against which opponents react with their own offers of an alternative ontology. Bazin's aesthetic presents one vocation for the cinema; it moves beyond description of an option to argue that illusionism is fundamentally the essence of cinema.[7] Consequently, in critiques of Bazin, a confusion of Bazinian theory with the Bazinian object occurs; in an unintentionally ironic way, the critique of reflection theory starts by believing that Bazin's theory reflects the cinema he examined because of a virtually iconic or even indexical connection between the two—in fact, Bazin's reading is no more than *a* reading.[8] That the classical American cinema is more than a representational cinema, and that Bazin himself found his theory straining at several points of contact with the Hollywood film,[9] seems to remain unrecognized by anti-illusionist critics who accept Bazin's argument at face value as a description of a real object: the whole of dominant cinema as an illusionist cinema.

Narrative and its ostensible canonization in Hollywood also become a target of recent criticism. For example, Noel Burch, in an interview in *Women and Film* (5/6), declares linearity—i.e., narrative progression—to be an, if not the, inherent code of what he sees as dominant cinema. In part, narrative is understood in such theory as little more than a form of illusionism; in line with Levi-Strauss's understanding of narrative in myth as that which is actually synchronic taking on the guise of the diachronic, the critique of narrative understands narrative development as the unveiling in time of what is really a continuity of space; narrative is seen as a fundamentally conservative form in which newly revealed moments are caught up by what has preceded them.[10] The story becomes, in such an approach, a fundamentally idealist form; a story unveils space: the depths which lie behind appearance. The narrative is a new example of a phenomenology, displayed like Hegel's across time, in which subjects and objects meet but only after a journey through dislocation.

Their connection to narrative explains why Barthes sees the hermeneutic and the proairetic codes—the codes of suspense and of action, respectively—as the most determined and determining codes of fiction. With both codes, a kind of narrative illusionism is seen to be at work. At a first narrative point, the text proposes an incomplete term which it promises at some later point to complete, to give a sense to. The hermeneutic and proairetic codes are (for Barthes) the only codes caught up in this game of incompleteness/completeness; while the symbolic code, especially, provides a plurality, a place where the text can be opened up, the hermeneutic and proairetic codes are committed by a force of logic to closure.

Against narrative and against transparency, critics and artists suggest a whole range of deconstructive practices. Many of these strategies are based on a notion of work, the necessity of an expenditure of labor in the reading of a text, so as to counteract the supposed ease and passivity of reading that narrative and transparency allow. Many recent critics push for a difficult art, an art that forces its audience into an active, interpretive response. The problem of passivity further provides the impetus for the rediscovery of Brecht, who has become, for recent critics, the master of deconstruction, the champion of formal subversion. Noel Burch, for example, in *Theory of Film Practice,* adopts Brecht's theory, but only after declaring it necessary to eliminate Brecht's concern for content.

Those elements (and, as I hope to demonstrate, they are no more than elements, altered when they are pulled out of context, and not the whole of the theory) which aid in a critique of illusionism and narrative are emphasized as the center of Brecht's theory. In *To the Distant Observer,* Burch valorizes the nonmatched cutting in many Japanese films (for example, the many cuts in Ozu's films *across* a 180-degree line) by an invocation of Brecht's theory of *gest.* In Burch's reading, the disjunctive editing of Japanese film subverts meaning by separating scenes from each other, an activity which Burch reads as parallel to the Brechtian understanding of the scene as a kind of tableau which foregrounds a *gest.* It is in such a reading that we can see the distorting powers of formalism. As Brecht describes the gestic effect, it is not simply a formal separation of scenes into tableaux but a separation so that each scene can present, in bold relief, a socially typical action. In Brecht's aesthetic, formal techniques are always in the service of social criticism, human comportment in everyday life held up to examination in light of the particular critical qualities of art. Roland Barthes suggests that the tableau effect—the cutting up of a narrative—may reconfirm specularity and containment; the individual scene can function like the "partial object" that is singled out from the whole body in acts of fetishism (Barthes, "Diderot, Brecht, Eisenstein," *Image/Music/Text*). (The way stills and eight-by-ten glossies can become partial-object substitutes for the experience of a film might serve as partial confirmation of Barthes's point.) Barthes's recognition that there is nothing inherently subversive about a tableau effect is an important one. For example, Lindsay Anderson's film *O Lucky Man!* (1975) demonstrates that an emphasis on tableaux can have variable meanings in a film. *O Lucky Man!* breaks up narrative flow in two different ways and to two different ends (although a formalism like Burch's would have to efface this difference). On the one hand, the film incorporates an often arbitrary usage of black frames inserted throughout the film. But far from calling into question the identificatory pleasures of the film, the black frames help confirm a pleasure in the film as film. That is, part of the pleasure of the text of *O Lucky Man!* is the way it confirms the magic of cinema (the characters who can pop up at any moment, the music that can start to play at any moment)—the sense of film as an ever-increasing offer of new experiences to the viewer—through a number of techniques including a disjunction played across technique (the black frames) as well as story (the hero, Mick Travis, goes from one adventure to another). On the other hand, certain scenes have a gestic force in their isolation from the body of the film; one such scene occurs for me when, having pronounced sentence in Mick's trial on trumped-up charges, the venerable judge returns to his chambers and strips down to participate in a flogging, in a scene set off from the film by black frames. Here the black frames isolate a particular action; the scene reflects back on the judge's venerability, qualifies it.

Brecht's theory is not an endorsement of a separation of elements or of the gestic technique or of epic construction *as such;* he continually emphasizes the particular ends to which theater must direct its craft and the need to remain open toward the value (or dis-value) of any particular means to those ends.

Brecht's oft-quoted example of a political gestic scene is that of a quarrel among the members of a working class family. A narrative of sorts is established: where will the quarrel lead, what kind of actions will ensue? The father begins to turn violent. Just then, a social worker enters, and the quarrelers freeze in the middle of their actions. This for Brecht is a social tableau. The fact that the action has stopped as such matters less than the fact that it has stopped in such a way as to pinpoint specific actions—that it has stopped to single out, amplify, demonstrate, the typicality of certain social gestures. In its capacity for social demonstration, such a scene would be very different from the formally similar freezing of action in, say, *Torn Curtain* (Alfred Hitchcock, 1966), where the fact that a ballerina recognizes a fugitive couple in the audience is indicated by freeze frames of the ballerina in her performance. The freeze frames jarringly disturb the narrative flow (and they disturb any *vraisemblable* of the scene); more than that, they offer up images of typical moments in a dance. But such a freeze is not a gest in Brecht's sense, since, here, typicality is not directly connected to the expression of a social attitude, to the political place and meaning of the character.

Brecht is not a formalist (nor is he a realist, pure and simple). Rather, as he explicitly argues, his goal is a *social* realism (in a sense of realism far different from, say, the social realism of Lukács); as he suggests in his essay, "Five Difficulties in Writing the Truth":

> It is not at all true that it is easy to find the truth. It is already not easy, first of all, to determine which truth it is worth writing about. It is true that at this moment, for example, all the great civilized nations are falling one after the other into barbarism. . . . This is undoubtedly a truth but there naturally exist many other truths. For example, it is not a falsity to say that chairs are made for sitting on and that rain falls from high to low. There are many writers who write about truths like that. (*Realisme*, p. 14)

Brecht clearly sees political art as a particular use of technique to bring out a particular social representation; one implication of this concern with such a specification of aesthetic processes is that a Brechtian art is programmatically political (although not dogmatically so). Political art does not simply come into being, but must be worked for, must be made. As Fredric Jameson explains:

> Brecht's aesthetic, and his ways of framing the problems of realism, are intimately bound up with a conception of science. . . . for Brecht, science is far less a matter of knowledge and epistemology than it is of sheer experiment and of practical, well-nigh manual activity. . . . it puts knowing the world back together with changing the world, and at the same time unites an ideal of praxis with a conception of production. . . . The spirit of realism designates an active, curious, experimental, subversive—in a word, *scientific*—attitude towards social institutions and the material world. ("Afterword," *Aesthetics and Politics*, 1977)

This kind of understanding of Brecht is very different from that which Burch uses in his reading of Japanese cinema, whereby artists can make a revolution without realizing it (and often in works whose subject matter is reactionary) simply by creating non-narrative, non-illusionist works. Formal innovation, legitimated in the aesthetic dimension, is easy to find, easy to describe, and so, at the cost of a repression, Brecht is enlisted in this operation. A new Brecht— Brecht the formalist—arises.

But there is also, and foremost, Brecht the social realist. Based on a reading far different from, and in many ways opposed to, the formalist reading of Brecht, I believe Brecht's aesthetic contains an important dialectical model for a political cinema, a cinema that would measure and represent the spectator's place in relation to that of art.

It is necessary here to anticipate a possible objection: namely, the potential distortion that could result from applying a theory of theater to the semiotically different art of film. Brecht's own attitude toward film—an attitude permanently shaped by the vicissitudes of his contact with the art—is indeed an ambivalent one. In his text on *The Threepenny Opera* lawsuit, Brecht sees cinema as *the* modern art, which the modern artist can avoid only at the cost of remaining a mere artisan, no longer in touch with the age: "Anybody who advises us not to make use of such new apparati just confirms the apparatus' right to do bad work. . . . At the same time he deprives us in advance of the apparatus we need in order to produce, since this way of producing is likely more and more to supercede the present one" (*Theatre,* p. 47). Brecht concludes that, "for film the principles of non-Aristotelean drama (a type of drama not depending on empathy, mimesis) are immediately acceptable." But almost ten years later, as he works in Hollywood on screenplays, Brecht directs what he refers to as a "fundamental reproach" to cinema. Writing in his *Arbeitsjournal* on 27 March 1942, Brecht argues that the cinema, in its inherent form, in the material nature of its signifying matter, is doomed to block critical intervention by the spectator:

> i don't believe that all technical problems are soluble in principle. in particular, i think that the effect of an artistic presentation on its spectators is not independent of the effect of the spectators on the arts. in the theatre, the audience regulates the performance. the film has monstrous weaknesses in detail which seem unavoidable in principle. . . . we only see what one eye, the camera, saw. this means that the actors have to act for this eye alone. . . . the mechanical reproduction gives everything the character of a result: the audience no longer has any opportunity to change the artist's performance. it is not assisting at a production, but at the end result of a production that took place in their absence. (Quoted in Ben Brewster, "The Fundamental Reproach," p. 44)

Brecht here joins with an essentialist way of seeing the cinema as an art inevitably consigned to encouraging spectator passivity, but the inadequacies of this reified view of the cinema and its supposed inability to involve spectators in anything more than a distant, specular relationship, have been recognized, not least by Brecht himself. Two factors, moreover, modify the initial intensity of Brecht's fundamental reproach. First, the fact that Brecht writes this particular entry while in Hollywood is not only a sign of his disaffection with Hollywood, but also, and conversely, a mark of his seriousness in posing the question of cinema as a question, not merely something to be dismissed. Significantly, Brecht makes a number of suggestions as to how that cinema can serve productive ends. He suggests as one possibility that *Hangmen Also Die,* a film he wrote for Fritz Lang in Hollywood, include gestic actions embodied in typical scenes which could be clipped out from the film, and used on their own for their (non-narrative) politically illustrative value. Second, Brecht's theory as a whole is directly opposed to any form of essentialist thinking. For Brecht, an art like cinema is fundamentally both regressive and progressive; that is, it is a material practice whose place in the social is never determinable in an a priori fashion. It was indeed the tendency to view the theater in reified terms that Brecht found so constraining in other critics and theorists of theatrical art. Theater, the theater Brecht holds up against cinema in his journal entry, is itself no essence, no unproblematically progressive form. As the bulk of his writings show, Brecht's own engagement with the politics of theater, with its materials, was an activity, a work, in which a matter (indeed, a resistant, reactive matter— the old theater; the moribund, bourgeois stage) had to undergo a reworking, a transformation, an alienation from its own alienating effects. Similarly, a Brechtian theory of cinema (present in fragments in Brecht's own writing) would view the cinema not as an essence but as a form, historically determined, which new kinds of cinema could change.

In his essay "The Fundamental Reproach (Brecht)" (*Cine-Tracts,* 1977), Ben Brewster suggests at least three different practices of a Brechtian aesthetic in cinema, all of which find explicit theoretical foundation in Brecht's writings. First, Brewster suggests that cinema can be made a critical form, one that truly involves spectator intervention, by a kind of literarization similar to that which Brecht calls for in his essay "The Literarization of the Theatre" (*Theatre,* pp. 43-47). There Brecht argues that what matters for political theater is not necessarily a mutual interaction between spectator and actor but an interaction *in* the spectator between two attitudes that he/she holds toward social comportment. Where such comportment usually passes unrecognized, epic theater has as its function, through the role of the actor, to add a voice to (i.e., to literarize) actions that are usually voiceless: "[This theatre] is a kind of report on life as any member of the audience would like to see. Since at the same time, however, he sees a good deal that he has no wish to see; since therefore he sees his wishes not merely fulfilled but also criticized (sees himself not as the subject but as the object), he is theoretically in a position to appoint a new function for the theatre" (p. 43). The actor here is little more than a kind of stage prop, surrendering psychological depth to facilitate criticism in the spectator's consciousness; indeed, Brecht's notion of the actor as influenceable by the spectator, which he uses to oppose theater to cinema, is one that plays little part in his developed aesthetic. (It is strongest in his early discussion of the *Lehrstuck*, the learning play, which the actors performed for themselves with no audience or in which the actors became their own audience.) In the essay "The Literarization of the Theatre," Brecht even goes so far as to suggest that certain kinds of plays might as well be read as seen; in this practice, one which would obviously banish the voice and presence of the actor, the spectator might be able to bring critical faculties to bear on the text in a way that the spectacular functions of performed theater might repress.

A literary cinema, similarly, would not be a cinema that one simply watched for the pleasure of sights and sound, but one that added a critical discourse to qualify those images. For theater, "literarizing entails punctuating 'representation' with 'formulation'; it gives the theatre the possibility of making contact with other institutions for intellectual activity" (pp. 43-44). One target here is spectacle. The spectacle form is a peremptory form which asserts to its spectators that all that is worthy of attention are signifiers on a screen and that the way such signifiers should be attended to is through a mere watching, a nonintellective acceptance of the meaningfulness of the spectacle image. In opposition to spectacle, literarization works to make art a discursive form, an arena of intellection and investigation. For example, in the film version of John Berger's *Ways of Seeing* (Michael Dibb, 1972), there is a constant literarization of two forms of art—painting and cinema. The film, which deals with the political functions of art, and attacks the Kenneth Clark type of documentary about art, does so not merely by talking about such art but by playing off the noncommunicability of art or the ambiguity of images against a discourse separate from *but juxtaposed with and against* those images. Berger argues at one point that oil painting helped the aristocracy to see their possessions, their success in power depicted. It is not just the narrator's distant voice which explains this but a direct intervention against such art; by means of a dissolve, the film adds to a Gainsborough portrait of a rich couple in their field the words "No trespassing." This addition of words to an image, brute though it may be, is a situating of the painting, an act of making the painting say something its appeal to mere spectacle had kept hidden. At the same time, the film deals with the potential danger of its own inclination as cinematic form toward spectacle; its solution is to offer itself as a kind of spectacle which the film then reveals to be a sham. Early sections of the film present Berger in extreme close-up against a neutral blue background, serving as narrator and doing so in the confident, convincing manner of an authority. Suddenly, the camera jumps back about fifty feet, to show Berger surrounded by film technology—lighting equipment, a false backdrop, sound equipment. The moment works to qualify Berger's authority, to indicate where that authority comes from. A film about aura, *Ways of Seeing* critiques the tendencies of film toward aura.

Brewster goes beyond literarization to suggest, as a second kind of audience/film dialectic, the work of various filmmaking groups that accompany their films at showings in order to turn the event of film watching into an event of film discussing. Here again, the cinema gives itself over to a kind of literarization, a speaking of its concerns, in which the film itself becomes no more than an object for qualification and examination. Work in video with its ease of recording and playback suggests a further development in this direction; Shirley Clarke's experiments in which groups record actions and then immediately look at and discuss what they have seen implies a kind of literarization that is every bit as nonpassive as that of theater.

Finally, and most suggestively, Brewster argues that to fully realize its goal, Brecht's *gest* would have to have recourse to the recording capabilities of film. Brecht imagined the most efficient use of *gest* to be what he called the *Pedagogium,* a museum that would store socially significant gests. This showroom of useful actions would be one that people could draw from to learn how to conduct their everyday lives. *Kuhle Wampe* (Slatan Dudow, 1932), the film Brecht worked on most fully, suggests a kind of primitive version of the pedagogium. An acted film, and thus more controlled at the pro-filmic level than a documentary, *Kuhle Wampe* nonetheless compiles a number of typical gestures of the German worker of the thirties: acts of despair (at not having a job); love and courtship; sports and cooperative endeavor. Indeed, as Brecht's report of the production team's unfavorable meeting with the German censor demonstrates, it is the nondocumentary quality of *Kuhle Wampe* that makes it typical, for the film is able to concentrate, to amplify, to pick out details (for example, a close-up that infuriated the censor shows a worker taking off his watch with an automatic and habitual gesture before commiting suicide by leaping from a window).

The construction of the film, moreover, allows the filmmakers to include scenes in which significant attitudes will bluntly appear (for example, in the final scene, members of all different classes and with all sorts of political positions find themselves in the same tram car discussing international politics). Brewster argues convincingly that a fully developed pedagogium could only be a *film* museum—a repository of actions indelibly recorded on celluloid. Indeed, the possibilities for film distribution and infinite replay of the same action give film certain advantages over theater in providing a wider audience for its epic procedures.

Given the dominance of misreadings of Brecht, it is perhaps necessary to specify what a Brechtian aesthetic is not. As I've suggested, the formalist reading of Brecht is based on a reading of dominant art as an art of illusionism and narrative closure. In an extreme version of this reading, the structural filmmakers argue that any film that includes filmed events is illusionist since it presents as present that which is really absent (the events filmed exist only in an anterior relation to the act of projection). Even when theorists do not go to the minimalist extreme of the structural filmmakers, their theories necessarily tend in a direction that valorizes a showing of the materiality of film. If illusion and narrative are repressive regardless of what is shown, regardless of what narrative developments occur, then the cinema itself as institution becomes the enemy. Whereas in earlier formalist critiques of cinema, certain types of film practice, which were supposedly alone in effecting a particular audience response (namely, passivity and uncritical receptivity), were singled out for critique, now the project of representation as a whole comes under scrutiny. In this view, the very structure of film viewing—audiences sitting before a screen and watching from a particular point of view or perspective—contributes to the constitution of the individual as a viewing subject—that is, as a subject safely elevated by self-confidence in a world reflected and represented on a screen, to a privileged, unchallenged position vis-à-vis the screen world. This rejection of representation suggests that attacks on the institution of cinema would have to come from totally nonrepresentational films; hence, the admiration of Le Grice or Burch for a film like Peter Kubelka's *Arnulf Rainier* (1957), a film of flickering black-and-white frames that would seem to allow little investment of the spectator's emotion. Anti-representational critics and artists push for new artistic experiences that call the traditional boundaries of the arts into question. But a set of overriding questions remains: in what ways is this undermining of accepted practices (if it is indeed an undermining, and if indeed these practices are the only accepted ones) a progressive, political one, and, more specifically, reflective of a Brechtian politics?

In part, of course, an answer depends on what we take the terms of the questions to mean. For example, Brecht understands political art as that which concerns itself with analyzing and then proposing strategies to deal with the contradictions of a particular historical situation. Obviously, formalist critics might claim that this is precisely what the art they support is doing. In the 1972 postscript to *Signs and Meanings in the Cinema,* Peter Wollen declares that a new art would cause the spectator to "produce fissures and gaps in the space of his own consciousness *(fissures and gaps which exist in reality but which are repressed by an ideology, characteristic of bourgeois society,* which insists on the 'wholeness' and integrity of each individual consciousness)" (p. 162, my emphasis). Wollen partially covers his tracks by declaring that such a repression is *characteristic* of and not necessarily omnipresent in bourgeois society, but the disclaimer itself is uncharacteristic of the radical formalist approach, which repeats any number of arguments about the passivity that popular art supposedly induces. The new aesthetic bases itself on a belief that texts lead to a domination of their subjects by placing those subjects in a particular position, physically, formally, perhaps ideologically. A text, in this sense, is an ensemble of codes that rationalize a particular way of relating to the world and then make this rationalizing attractive by not interfering with the fetishistic or voyeuristic perspective of the viewing subject. In his essay, "The Politics of Separation," Colin MacCabe goes so far as to call this seduction "the bribe of identity," thereby situating textual persuasion in the realm of crime.

This sort of position leaves many points unanswered or at least ambiguous. Before we can assess the validity of certain subversive strategies as answers, we need to make sure that the problem has been correctly understood. We need to examine the notion of textual domination. Such a notion rests on two fundamental points: that texts confirm the world and blind us to contradictions, and that submission to a text means submission to an ideological practice. The belief in a bribe of identity sees the text as a complicity of codes, a rhetoric that hides its own rhetorical nature. Thus, critics like MacCabe see the text as a force of domination over spectators.

But all texts dominate. Without a degree of code sharing between art-makers and art-receivers, the artwork would become a kind of noise. To alter MacCabe's economic metaphor (which he obviously doesn't intend as a metaphor), texts aren't bribes; they are contracts in which spectators or readers willingly agree to relate to codes in a certain way and, I would contend, usually with knowledge of the workings of many of these codes. The signs of the contract appear throughout the texts; they may become familiar to us precisely because they are signs. We have to learn them to be able to read or to view. And yet submission to a contractual promise is only one side of the working of a text. As information theory suggests, communication ceases not only without a certain adherence to codes; it also, in contrast, ceases if there is nothing but redundancy, repetition of the initial communication: there must be a certain (controlled) transgression. Art, all art, bases itself not just on confirmation but also on a necessary contradiction of forms. Frank Kermode has described this interplay alternatively as one between credulity and skepticism (in *The Sense of an Ending*) and one between recognition and deception ("Novels: Recognition and Deception," *Critical Inquiry,* 1974). To a large extent, the self-reflexivity that new criticism valorizes in certain texts represents no more than one strategy in the interplay of a process intrinsic to *and actually defining the aesthetic dimension.* One sort of pleasure comes from precisely this interplay of credulity and skepticism; part of the appeal of self-reflexive art is that it heightens this intrinsic interplay.

If we survey the development of the literary and dramatic arts, we continually come across examples of art which signal awareness of their own artifice. Literary critics often point to *Tristram Shandy* as a highpoint in the conscious use of artifice; in a revealing comment, Viktor Shklovsky called it "the most typical novel in world literature." Such a comment does not so much indicate the uniqueness of the book, its separation from the mass of the literature, but the ways in which it makes explicit, foregrounds, a *nature* of literature. Indeed, as an eighteenth-century novel, Fielding's *Tom Jones* goes almost as far as Sterne's book in uncovering the codes that a reading of literature depends on. Fielding, for example, explicitly invokes the model of a contract by comparing the novel to a meal where there is a certain interplay between the fixed, promised order of courses and the changing identities of the foods in that order. The difference between *Tristram Shandy* and *Tom Jones,* at the level of their play with codes, is one of degree, not of kind; it is a modification, not a break. Invocations of the classic novel in formalist criticism construct a mythic version of such a novel in which many of the qualities of that literature are repressed or ignored.

The development, to continue this example, of the English novel from Sterne to Joyce (and beyond) is a development (in a far from linear fashion) of a tendency and characteristic in the novel as an aesthetic form. But formalist criticism, by its very premises, can have little room for a recognition of degrees; its thinking is in terms of breaks. Barthes, for example, has suggested that modernism was not really a possibility for art until 1850; he thereby ignores the fact that every artistic period is necessarily an interplay between tradition and artistic revolution.

Revealingly, humanist literary and art criticism has long been able to accommodate transgressions of the rules of the communication act.[11] The usual approach is to see such transgressions as necessary to a progress that otherwise would stultify. Establishment critics have long been able to situate modernism in a nonrevolutionary aesthetic. One can cite many examples of this accommodation. Two books of literary analysis—Robert Alter's *Partial Magic* (1975) and Albert Guerard's *The Triumph of the Novel* (1976)—have as their goal to read a tradition of literature in an antirealist way (Guerard, for example, includes Dickens in a tradition of Dostoievski and Faulkner, against the traditional reading of Dickens as painter of society). Both authors celebrate what they coincidentally call "the Great Other Tradition," thereby expanding the canon beyond the limits prescribed by Leavis. Both Guerard and Alter (and these are only two examples) transform aesthetic disturbances into positive, humanist values. More precisely, they recognize literary or formal innovation for what it often is: a nonthreatening, typical component of art and of its appeal. Guerard, for example, refers to the novel's powers of "illuminating and imaginative distortion," thus recognizing qualities that formalist political criticism can only find in a few, select works. Literature can introduce an imbalance for the purpose of establishing a higher balance; the term *avant-garde* literally suggests nothing more than an advance force.

Viktor Shklovsky argued for art as *ostranenie,* a making strange of the world. And indeed if art confirms, it also makes strange the normal order of things. Suspension of belief accompanies suspension of disbelief. All art is distanced. This is as true of Hollywood as of Laurence Sterne or Aristophanes. We learn to read through this distance, but we also learn to want new distances.

Hollywood not only presents unreality as reality; it openly acknowledges its unreality. In his book, *America in the Movies* (1975), Michael Wood goes so far as to suggest that unreality can become the condition of Hollywood film. Campiness, he argues, is not an aspect of some entertainment films, but the very condition of entertainment; as he says, "Hollywood is the only place in the world where anyone says, 'Santa Maria, it had slipped my mind!'"

The Hollywood cartoon—a staple of Hollywood production—embodies many of the formal techniques claimed to be deconstructive. And yet if any *political* concern can be claimed for most of these cartoons, this is so only in the etymological sense of political as that which deals with the *polis*, with "universal" relations of people to each other: the stories of the cartoons reject history (except for moments which intrude like a veritable return of a repressed), and their formal innovations work not to "produce fissures and gaps" but to reconfirm the spectator's faith in the entertainment value of cinema.

Brecht argues that artworks differ not so much in their degree of formal complexity as in their representation of political attitudes, in their use of form to highlight certain attitudes about the world. An analysis of a typical cartoon will bear this out. *Duck Amuck* (Chuck Jones, 1953) is a virtual culmination of the experimental possibilities of the Hollywood cartoon. The subject of the cartoon is the nature of animation technique itself. In *Duck Amuck,* Daffy Duck undergoes victimization at the hand of his animator, ultimately revealed to be none other than Bugs Bunny. Bugs tortures Daffy by playing with such film coordinates as framing, background, and color. In an article on *Duck Amuck* in *Film Comment* (1975), Rick Thompson rightly notes that the film manifests a high degree of emphasized formal complexity: "the film is extremely conscious of itself as an act of cinema, as is much of Jones's work.... *Duck Amuck* is a good example of Noel Burch's dialectic idea of film elements: foreground and background, space and action, character and environment, image and soundtrack are all in conflict with one another...."
Yet Burch's dialectic idea, as he himself admits (*Theory of Film Practice*, p. xix), is far from a Marxist dialectic, and so is *Duck Amuck*. If *Duck Amuck* becomes a metaphor for the confusions of life (as Thompson suggests) it is a disengaged metaphor at best, since it suggests only certain forms of this confusion, and certain causes. Indeed, the source of Daffy Duck's angst reveals itself to be none of the agents of social domination in a real world, but merely Bugs Bunny—another fictive character, whose power is tautological in source. The film opens up a formal space, and not a political one, in viewer consciousness, and so ultimately does not subvert but confirms. *Duck Amuck* closes in on itself, fiction leading to and springing from fiction, the text becoming a loop that effaces social analysis.

We may approach this issue from another direction if we examine those theories that deal with traditional art's supposed function vis-à-vis the daily workings of the everyday world. Recent critics contend, as the earlier quote from Peter Wollen suggests, that bourgeois art works to instill a complacency in the viewer, a complacency both about the art object itself and about the world outside of art. But there is nothing necessarily consoling or optimistic about bourgeois art. Nor is life under capitalism necessarily one of complacency and isolation from an awareness of contradiction. It depends on what kind of contradiction and what kind of awareness we're talking about. That our day-to-day expectations can be thwarted is a normal and accepted possibility of everyday life. The conventional work of art does not banish contradiction; rather, it works by divorcing contradiction from its social context and cause. Everyday life is often little more than a continual succession of disappointments, of subversions, all of which fissure our self unity and social unity as acting subjects. Art does not deny this malaise; it merely hides and denies its roots in historical forces. This is why contemporary culture can well accommodate formally subversive art; as long as such art does not connect its formal subversion to an analysis of social situations, such art becomes little more than a further example of the disturbances that go on as we live through a day. And a work of art that defeats formal expectations does not lead to protest against a culture that deals continually in the defeating of expectations. This may help to explain the morbid underside of fan fascination with Hollywood— an underside of scandal magazines and, ultimately, of the elevation of trash books like Kenneth Anger's *Hollywood Babylon,* with its photos of Jayne Mansfield's car crash and of Judy Garland strung out on drugs, to coffee table respectability. We are used to having our realities deconstructed to such an extent that we may even ask for such a deconstruction, and so too, it does not bother us to see the reality of the movie screen world deconstructed. In her article *Mary Hartman, Mary Hartman* in *Socialist Revolution* (1976), Barbara Ehrenreich suggests that the TV series represents the triumph of contradiction: a show that attacks the consumer world is sponsored to sell the very sort of products its content disdains. And it succeeds. Ehrenreich presents this plenitude of contradictions as a stumbling block to leftist theories of popular culture, which in the past took the form of a manipulation theory. If it were merely a question of art inspiring blind optimism, criticism would be easy, as it has been for formalism. Shows like *Mary Hartman, Mary Hartman* have made pessimism, discontent, and irony marketable. What a radical aesthetics needs to deal with is this realm of contradiction which obscures political contradictions.

And here we return to Brecht. Brecht also sees a difference and distance between art and political art. Art, he argues, automatically embodies a distancing, a making strange. But there's nothing yet socially distancing about that. Brecht continually emphasizes the ways in which bourgeois theater has become acceptable to audiences despite its strangeness to them; in the bourgeois theater, for example, the worker sees images of life that have little to do with his/her life. This is the destiny of art under capitalism. In opposition to this "natural" destiny, Brecht argues that to be progressive art has to be made so; what has become habitual—the marketability of alienation—has to be disturbed.

In his essay "The Modern Theatre is the Epic Theatre," Brecht uses the example of opera to present his conception of art as possessing *intrinsic* qualities of distance from reality, to which the artist can *add* a sense of political engagement. As is well known, Brecht's theory of art reception emphasizes conscious knowledge over intuition. So does his theory of art creation. Like his teacher, Erwin Piscator, Brecht sees art as filling a *programmed* function. This implies conscious attention to form and to content.

Brecht reportedly discovered the alienation effect when actors at a rehearsal for *Edward II* began to get tired and to approach their roles with a distanced, uninvolved attitude. But, even if its roots are in accidents of this sort, Brecht's aesthetic is a constant attempt to develop control of art, to merge art and the rational, indeed to make the production of art a rational activity. Political art, for Brecht, is not just a matter of formal innovation (a potential he sees open to all artists) but of a particular view of society that is not available by intuition or accident but only by work and investigation, a scientific attitude. Summing up the problem of nonrationalistic theories of artistic production, Brecht puts the matter bluntly: "[According to intuitionist aesthetics] the act of the artist happens unconsciously, he is somnabulistic, he doesn't even know his own motivations, he obeys inspirations, and he doesn't demand that one understand him but merely identify with him. This is the famous definition of art according to which an artist can be great while being an idiot" ("Self-Criticism," *Réalisme*, p. 78).

This emphasis on planning probably most separates Brecht from Lukács's position, which seems to favor an intuitionist approach to literary creation: "Lasting typologies based on a perspective of this sort [i.e., based on the "selection of the essential and the subtraction of the inessential"] owe their effectiveness not to the artist's understanding of day-to-day events but to his unconscious possession of a perspective independent of and reaching beyond his understanding of the contemporary scene" (*Realism in Our Time*, p. 57). Lukács's belief in unconscious awareness leads Brecht to call him a formalist, for it is precisely a belief like Lukács', that the nineteenth-century masters had the answers and that these answers are still relevant to the twentieth century, which keeps literary production in the realm of accident and signals a refusal to situate such production within the actual workings of history.

In fact, Brecht's aesthetic suggests that we need to expand and clarify the notion of realism. Significantly, Brecht refers to his own artistic project as a realism. Realism, he suggests, is no more (and no less) than a type of attitude toward the world. Brecht's theory most significantly distinguishes between realism—which he saw as the overriding impulse of his art—and unrealism, the setting up of false or limited or reified attitudes toward the world and toward worldly possibilities, whether these be attitudes of a formalist art or a naturalist one. In his essay "The Popular and the Real," Brecht defines realism as "discovering the causal complexes of society unmasking the prevailing view of things as the view of those who rule." Realism is thus a form of knowledge, a picturing of reality. To judge the efficacy of a particular realism, "one must compare the depiction of life in a work with the life that is being depicted." Like the Lacanian theory of the subject that formalist criticism draws upon, Brecht's theory depends on a notion of positioning, of the subject's place in the circuit of communication. But Brecht diverges from this theory in an important way. For Brecht, the attitudinal position of the viewing subject springs from an attitudinal position in the work (in the social content and form of the work and not just in its systems of address, as Colin MacCabe's reading of Brecht would have it); the political artwork embodies a difference between the way things are and the way they can be. Brecht's formal experimentation depends on subject matter in two ways. Form must change in relation to changing subjects; otherwise, Brecht argues, the formalism of a Lukács, in which a certain form of the novel works in all times, will result. Second, Brecht's political theater is a theater of possibility—a theater showing that life doesn't only have to take on the forms that it generally does. Theodor Adorno suggests that this opens a Brechtian aesthetic up to the danger of a voluntarist attitude toward political engagement: it is finally up to the artist to decide what is real, what isn't, what is changeable about reality, what isn't. Adorno declares:

> Brecht wanted to reveal in images the inner nature of capitalism. In this sense his aim was indeed what he disguised it as against Stalinist terror—realistic. But this burdened him with the obligation of ensuring that what he intended to make unequivocally clear was theoretically correct. His art, however, refused to accept this *quid pro quo*: it both presents itself as didactic, and claims aesthetic dispensation from responsibility for the accuracy of what it teaches. ("Commitment," *Aesthetics and Politics,* p. 183)

But what Adorno presents as a shortcoming of the Brechtian aesthetic has to be seen as a problem and an issue: the relation of any artwork to social action will always have a certain voluntaristic or indeterminate quality. Indeed, Adorno's aesthetic—the negative dialectic in which the work of Beckett or Schönberg or Joyce, among others, takes a distance from the loss of social life under capitalism, and so becomes a negation of negation—can only present itself as an objective, true politics of art by ignoring a whole set of historicizing questions (for example, the question of reception, which Adorno can only read in terms of a high art/low art split).

If there is a certain formalism to Brecht's project—an attention to techniques first, and only afterwards attention to the ways techniques might engage with history—this is the inevitable formalism of any art, the edge of unpredictability of certain effects when they enter into real historical situations.

Brecht's interest in experimentation, his strictures against any too rigidly constructed theory of political art, are so many attempts to minimize unpredictability and keep art open to the changing demands of history.

If there is one characterization of political art which does not change throughout Brecht's writing, it is his definition of a political art as one that compares an image of human beings as "unalterable" to an image of them as "alterable and able to alter" ("The Modern Theatre is the Epic Theatre"). As such, the new theater shows that formal arrangements of life can change. We can do things we never thought possible, not the least of these being to challenge the universality of bourgeois thought and practice. But not all possibilities are equally valid. Brecht defers (at the point that Adorno would see as voluntarist) to extra-aesthetic criteria: what is valid is what will lead to a worker's socialism. Indeed, if there is an idealist side to Brecht's aesthetic, it is not so much in his voluntarism, but in his conception of the worker as a full individual, able to recognize progressive art when he/she has the chance. Brecht's theory often defers to an unexamined, undialectical vision, not unlike Lukács's, of the worker as the virtually automatic carrier of history:

> The workers judged everything as to the truth of its content; they welcomed every innovation which helped the representation of truth, of the real mechanism of society; they rejected everything that seemed theatrical, technical equipment that merely worked for its own sake.... There will always be people of culture, connoisseurs of art, who will interject: 'Ordinary people do not understand that [experimentation].' But the people will push these persons impatiently aside and come to a direct understanding with artists. ("The Popular and the Real," *Brecht*, pp. 110-11)

Brecht's theory, then, is ultimately a theory with ambiguous connections to practice: his conception of the worker, for example, lacks a necessary understanding of psychology, of the ways one might go against self-interest and conscious intent. Again, though, this is not so much a full criticism of Brecht as a recognition of the inevitable incompleteness of any theory of art in the face of historical applications of aesthetic practice. Brecht's theory, though inspired and influenced by his practice, is precisely a theory, a generalization.

For Brecht, political art plays off of a political redefinition of credulity and skepticism. If the new world of social possibility is not to appear as nothing but noise, a too-new newness, the artwork must also make use of the old world as a standard. Meaning, and its realization in action, comes from the differences between the two worldviews present(ed) in the artwork. Political art defamiliarizes the world. But it can only do so by playing off of our connections to that world. As a realism, the Brechtian aesthetic uses formal techniques, a play with the specific codes of art, in the service of encouraging comment on and criticism of a given social reality. The function of distantiation techniques is not so much to remind the spectators that they are watching a play or a film (since they already are aware of that) but to break down the socially unquestioning way that people watch spectacle. The separation of elements (for example, of actors from their roles, of mise-en-scène from story, of props from the setting, directs attention to aspects of a performance, of a spectacle, which are missed when all elements are working together. As in the notion of *ostranenie* so dear to Russian formalism, a separation of elements makes those elements strange, pinpoints them, but since art itself is already strange, a kind of disengagement from the real complexity of social phenomena, Brecht argues that it is ultimately, but primarily, social comportment that should be made strange in art, through a kind of negation of the negation that the aesthetic dimension is.

As Brecht's writings reveal, the need to quote acts of social comportment, to frame them, as it were, and make them available for criticism, can take on two different forms. On the one hand, the theater can serve as a place where comportment in everyday life outside the theater can be criticized. The estranging devices will, in this case, work to pull social actions from their habitual framework, a framework that because it is habitual allows these acts to pass unremarked or unexamined. At the same time, in its new context, the action must still bear signs of its original context; the audience must recognize that the action they are seeing on the stage is not just an action that occurs in the fictive world of the theater but one that has an extratheatrical referent. Robert Nelson's *O Dem Watermelons* (1965), a film acted by the Brechtian San Francisco Mime Troupe, is a Brechtian film in this sense, using its techniques to make comportment by whites toward blacks criticizable (the film was used as an organizing tool during NAACP marches in the 1960s). Through its chronicle of watermelons, which late in the film are associated with blacks, the film works to first encourage a seemingly innocent spectatorial pleasure—the film starts out as an eccentric oddity allowing destructive fantasies to play themselves out. The function of the film's progression is to increasingly politicize this innocence, to qualify it.

But, at the same time, since art consumption—for example, theater-going—is itself a form of social comportment, Brecht's aesthetic also suggests a making strange of aesthetic events themselves. A Brechtian art of this sort would distance the normal conditions in which art is received to suggest the social implications of the ostensibly normal reception. It is this direction in Brecht's writing—the concern with self-reflexivity—that formalist interpretations of Brecht have latched onto. However, as I've tried to suggest, their interpretation fails, due to a reductive and restrictive misunderstanding of what "normal" spectating conditions are; these readings consequently end up valorizing as exceptional that which is really and finally acceptable as part of tradition. Contrary to formalism, Brecht understands progressive formal art not as a polyphony or a complication of perspective, but as a cutting through of obfuscations—whether the complications of modernist art or the simplicities of naturalism—to put into art that which it tries to cover up: a representation of the values and meanings of social acts. In this sense, we can well imagine a combination of Brecht's two approaches to political art, since it is its refusal of political subject matter—of nontheatrical, socially typical *gests*—that is the social typicality of the theater.

In this sense, a film like Bruce Conner's *Report* (1963-65) can seem a Brechtian film, revealing myths about the Kennedy aura but also including cinematic presentation itself as one of the forms of that aura. After CBS refused him footage of the Kennedy assassination, Conner made a film about the film by editing together footage of everything but that event. We see Kennedy arriving in Dallas; we see the car driving toward Dealy Plaza; we see the funeral procession after the death. This is a diachronic slice in which the central element is absent. At the same time, Conner presents a synchronic picture, alternating events from Dallas with pop images culled from American life; we see a refrigerator commercial, a telephone operator, clips from an old war movie. At the moment of the assassination (heard on the soundtrack, which is composed entirely of radio broadcasts), the screen goes blank and then into a flicker-effect (alternating black-and-white frames). With images of anything but the assassination, and with the total absence of images, *Report* plays on our customary attitude, our desire to see an event like an assassination. Conner's film suggests that we can never know the event but only media presentations of it; as if to show how reality is constructed by media, several scenes are loop-printed and run over and over again to suggest that an event can be postponed, effaced, by the way it is presented. *Report* takes a typical moviegoing desire and quotes it through a critical stance. In one loop-printing, the car moves toward its destination but is bounced back by the editing. The next shots are from the synchronic presentation; this, *Report* shows us, is the real event, not the documentary payoff our habits of viewing have led us to want from films promising to be "about" the Kennedy assassination.

This reading of Brecht has two important implications for our discussion. First of all, the fact that political art plays off of pre-political art suggests that if the political text invites production from the spectator, this production is a source of pleasure. Significantly, pleasure and the importance of artistic popularity come under attack in much of the new radical criticism (see, for example, Martin Walsh's defense in *Jump Cut* 4 of the theoretical rigor and difficulty of the films of Straub and Huillet). In this work we witness the rise of a break or gap between criticism and popular reception, a break that is a misreading of Brecht's theory as a theory of difficulty. It is in this misreading of Brecht (as in MacCabe's comparison of Joyce and Brecht) that all of the values that Brecht upholds for political art, except formal experimentation, disappear. In reading the use a writer like MacCabe makes of Brecht one would never imagine that Brecht supported realism (the theater as a demonstration of something);

pleasure (the theater as a joyous confirmation of the changeability of the world); popularity (a theater that works for the working classes). Significantly, Brecht constantly argued that the mass audience had to decide the validity of a formal experiment. Moreover, he displayed a continued faith in a mass audience's ability to accept—and more than that, to demand—new forms for the theater: "The means must be asked what the end is. The people know how to ask this.... The workers judged everything by the amount of truth contained in it; they welcomed any innovation which helped the representation of truth.... 'You can't mix theatre and film': that sort of thing was never said" ("The Popular and the Realistic," *Théatre,* p. 110).

Although the new readings of Brecht situate themselves in opposition to humanist criticism, they paradoxically invoke a division of taste parallel to the high culture/mass culture distinction so beloved in humanist criticism. From Ortega y Gasset's dehumanization of art to Susan Sontag's erotics of art to Roland Barthes's distinction between pleasure and bliss, there is little change in the formalist endeavor. Recent critics present themselves as possessing a heightened aesthetic understanding while the masses supposedly stumble along in realist and narrative naivete. At worst, this approach refuses history; it regards a certain popular sort of viewing practice as debased and quotidian, and so dismisses it, refusing to examine the contradictory stance of mass culture.

Brecht's examination of pleasure and popularity suggests that we need to distinguish between at least three sorts of aesthetic pleasure. There is the pleasure of familiarity. This is the pleasure of uncritical, reified realism, the seeing of the world in the ways it has always been seen. Then there is the pleasure that comes from art's dehumanization or from forced self-reflexivity, which I've suggested is little different from the first register of pleasure. This is the pleasure of art as form, as aesthetic emotion in the Kantian sense. This is a pleasure that, as Barthes contends in *Pleasure of the Text,* derives its force from its avoidance of history, by aestheticizing or textualizing it. Then there is the pleasure argued for by Brecht, the pleasure of an art that finally realizes the dream of Horace in his *Ars Poetica* (which Brecht continually refers to): to please and instruct; to please through instruction; to instruct through pleasure. This is an art whose content is a combination of the world and a better version of that world.

As a consequence of this attitude toward pleasure, Brecht's theory raises a second implication for political art. Insofar as Brecht's political art includes the presence of the familiar world and yet presents a more attractive world, Brechtian art is initially an art of identification. The spectator must identify with the old for its criticism by the new to have any force. In analyzing Brecht's theory, critics have too often declared that the theories allow no place for identification. In fact, Brecht distinguishes several types of identification (just as he distinguished several types of pleasure): there is an empathetic and unquestioning identification—the one connected to a reified vision of the world and a reified art (whether realist or modernist), and a critical one—a new perspective of knowledge from which the old way is scrutinized. In his essay "Alienation Effects in Chinese Acting," Brecht is emphatic about the need for identification in political theater: "the audience identifies itself with the actor as being an observer, and accordingly develops his attitude of observing or looking on" (*Theatre,* p. 93). As Brecht emphasized in his writings, there is no one form that best meets the requirements of progressive art. Concentrating on ways to unveil what is representative in real social relations, never disdaining the need for widespread appeal and for the pleasure that audiences can feel in realizing the relativity of what they had assumed to be permanent, the Brechtian aesthetic is an important and vital one. But a necessary first step, one that I have tried to provide here, is simply to understand that aesthetic, to extract this theory so opposed to the stasis of formalism from a new formalism that in claiming to understand Brecht, ironically threatens to freeze the Brechtian approach in a stasis of its own.

Oshima's Political Art

"We must start from zero."
"No. Before starting from zero, we must go back to zero."
Emile and Patrice in Godard's *Le gai savoir*

Three times in Nagisa Oshima's *Night and Fog in Japan* (1960) there is a freeze-frame of several participants in the last-night demonstration by the Japanese left against ratification of the Japanese-American accords. The film literally comes to a stop. Each of these static moments is followed by a cut to whiteness (revealed by subsequent camera movement to be the sheet on a hospital bed). In this arrestment of action and in the way that the film repetitively cycles back to a pivotal moment in modern Japanese history, *Night and Fog in Japan* suggests the problems of political and cultural struggle as it focuses on a number of radicals and former radicals who confront the past they have never really gotten beyond. Story—the narrative of these radicals—joins with political style: here, the flashbacks that forcefully invoke the past and represent the dictum that to ignore the past condemns one to repeating it.[1]

Night and Fog in Japan also raises the question of *repetition* as a problem for the political filmmaker: how does a filmmaker encounter tradition and what is the relation between the weight of tradition and the potential for cultural innovation? In *Night and Fog in Japan,* Oshima presents political filmmaking as a kind of return to zero, to use Godard's famous phrase from *Le gai savoir.* Filmmaking is here a kind of wiping clean of that slate (in this case, the movie screen) upon which things are inscribed; the cuts to white are so many returns to an initial condition of cinema, an emptiness that the filmmaker must fill in. Each time the screen goes white, one narrative comes to an end and another stutters into existence.

But in this early film, Oshima views the possibilities for progress—in film, in politics, and in film politics—with a certain pessimism. The repeated attempts to initiate a future that will leave behind tradition's weight are repressed by a stronger repetition; the film, which began by a camera movement out of the darkness and obscurity of a foggy night into a room where a marriage is taking place, ends by moving back out of that room to an outside that has become even foggier and more obscure. Not yet dominant in Oshima's filmmaking is that sense that will come to inform the techniques of certain of his later films: it is the spectator, living a history of the present, faced with a real future, who has the ability to move beyond the limitations—the fictions—of the cinematic signifier. In *Realm of the Senses,* especially, one can read the practice of Oshima's cinema as dialectical in a forceful way: the cinema is no longer an art of viewers merely watching a complete(d) story, but a practice of spectators as historical subjects, in situation, asked to bring their own critical reactions to bear on the world of the film, asked to use the film as a raw material, a given representation of history. The film becomes a pre-text—what Sartre refers to in the *Critique de la raison dialectique* as a *totalité,* an image of history as a stopped and fixed entity, that through active intervention can give way to a *totalization,* an ongoing reworking of pretexts by a critical activity. Viewing becomes an active process in which spectator and cinema meet in a dialogical encounter in which both are changed. The spectator judges his/her own historical situation against that of the film, and in so doing learns to think of situations as historical. Across Oshima's career, *Realm of the Senses* repeats *Night and Fog in Japan* but it is a repetition with an important difference: although both films are about the seeming insecurity of an inside (rooms, ceremonial sites) into which an historical outside intrudes, *Realm of the Senses* suggests that what intrudes is not only a past history, captured in the film (the 1936 which, as an end voice-over tells us, is the setting of the action), but more than that, the spectator's own place in a history that is external to the happenings of the story. Oshima's film suggests that film politics is not simply a matter of the politics of a represented content. Rather, politics is a question of the spectator's place as spectator. In particular, *Realm of the Senses* blocks identification with characters to encourage the spectator's evaluation of the characters' situation and their response to it. This evaluation is also potentially an evaluation of filmgoing itself, since filmgoing traditionally seems to encourage identification.

This is not to suggest that *Realm of the Senses* automatically succeeds as political art while *Night and Fog in Japan* automatically fails. In fact, if *Night and Fog in Japan* seems to minimize the intervening critical work of the spectator to the advantage of an articulated presentation of a rich political content, *Realm of the Senses* seems to proceed in an opposite direction: political content—the qualification by the film of represented events as political—is muted, marginalized. Indeed, much of the political sense of the film depends upon the spectator's prior knowledge of references in the film (for example, what 1936 represents or what the place of the geisha district in Tokyo was); whereas *Night and Fog in Japan* does all the work, moving the spectator to a conclusion that the film proffers as inevitable. *Night and Fog in Japan* makes few connections explicit and so runs the risk of treating the spectator's role as one of a purely formal or playful freedom. The film addresses the spectator as a subject, but there is a tendency for the address of this spectator to slide from an historical to a psychological or existential one (the brute presence of the sex and blood as somehow "outside" history or "beyond" or more "immediate" than history and politics). Significantly—and reversing any simple, teleological view of Oshima as an artist who discovers a pure blend of political style and subject—Oshima's next film, *Realm of the Passions,* made as a complement to *Realm of the Senses,* is a return to the style of the earliest films, tinged with a pessimism similar to that of *Night and Fog in Japan.* Both films suggest the inability of characters to transcend the givens of their existence (for example, with the hero and heroine killed by the authorities, the last shot of *Realm of the Passions* shows the hero's idiot brother dancing endlessly and meaninglessly in a snowfall). But unlike *Night and Fog in Japan, Realm of the Passions* does not have a political issue as its subject (except for the very end with the authorities' entrance on the scene); the latter film is a love story understood in romantic and virtually mystical terms (the film as resurrection of that most enduring Japanese genre, the ghost story). As a ghost story, *Realm of the Passions* imagines the distinction of inside and outside world in terms of an opposition of love and the supernatural; the police officer who comes to the village to inquire about the disappearance of the murdered husband, and the townspeople who ultimately torture and put to death the hero and heroine, are pictured as so many "agents" of the supernatural forces, of a kind of divine, albeit misguided, justice.

It is rather in *Death by Hanging* (1968), his most evidently Brechtian film, that Oshima deals explicitly with the question of the social definition of the human subject. *Death by Hanging* shows the definition of that subject in bourgeois thought and its contradiction by an historically open definition, one that pinpoints how each human being's identity is in great part an effect of social codings. In this film, when a condemned man's body refuses to die, the officials of the state find themselves forced to define what the individual is as defined inside and outside the law. Again, like the other films, *Death by Hanging* is structured around an opposition between an enclosed inside, a site of deception and non-self-examination, and an historically reflexive outside. The officials find that their attempts to give the prisoner, R, an identity, require them to look at the outside world and to admit all the (previously unadmitted) determinants that go into making up identity and individuality. Moreover, by strategies of involvement that give way to distantiation, the film causes the spectator to go through a similar process, calling into question the security of simplistic ways of seeing.

In these three films, then, Oshima's cinema can exemplify the search for a new kind of political cinema, one committed not simply to the representation of politics on screen but to the enactment of politics as a process between screen and spectator. In many ways, Oshima seems to set out to continue, improve, and, perhaps, put into active play the project that Eisenstein had set out forty years earlier. Like Eisenstein, Oshima starts from zero, rejecting documentary solutions as misleading (for example, as in the opening of *Death by Hanging,* which is exemplary in this respect), and trying to build up a new set of techniques in order to relate to spectators in new ways; for example, the interaction of camera movement and debate by characters in *Night and Fog in Japan* echoes the interaction between technique and representations that is central to Eisenstein's project. For Oshima (as for Eisenstein), the politics of cinema lies not only in what one sees but in how one sees. In short, Oshima is searching for a *rhetorical* cinema in which the process of figuration implicates the spectator. In his proposed film of *Kapital,* Eisenstein hoped to reproduce the nature of dialectics in the ways that spectators would produce the sense of the film. In a film like *Death by Hanging,* Oshima aspires to make the spectator understand the powers of a new form of cinema by literally embedding an old cinema—that of documentary with its particular ways of seeing—into the film. Like Eisenstein, Oshima is searching for a rhetorical cinema, a cinema in which the processes of figuration implicate the spectator, and that is itself nothing without that spectator.

Oshima's cinema investigates not only the personal but the political, and the various ways that relationships between them can be articulated. The opening shot of *Night and Fog in Japan*—a single, ten-minute travelling shot—reveals, by its very movement, one way in which this relationship can exist. Without cutting, the camera brings new realities into its view, suggesting that these realities exist together, that there is a *link* between the personal and the political. Thus, from the dark and swirling fog, the camera moves inexorably into the students' compound where a marriage ceremony is taking place. Whereas the foggy outside is a space of ambiguity and indistinguishability, the space of the wedding, with its ceremonial rigidity, appears at first as the embodiment of clarity and certainty. But the course of the film, a course often literally figured by camerawork, will suggest that this interior world can only achieve its security by ideological distortion and reduction: political struggle has to become a thing of the past, repressed, literally pushed outside. For instance, only certain people—those deemed safe and politically unadventurous—have been invited to the wedding of these former radicals.

What the film enacts is a return of the politically repressed in which the camera movement, tracking with two uninvited radicals as they enter the room, is itself part of the critique. The pivoting and circling camera works against the symmetry of the wedding scene—bride and groom in center, and guests in rows on each side—and suggests that that symmetry has no basis other than the reifications of a social ceremony. The wedding ritual would appear to be a ceremony of clarity and reason, an escape from the darkness of political confusion. In contrast, in a political struggle that has not yet found a sense of direction, the world of struggle and of history doesn't seem at first to have any real existence or foundation. Consequently, we never really see the outside; instead, one close-up stands as an emblematic sign (in a virtually Brechtian sense) for the whole of the arena of political struggle, which is presently only a drama of isolated faces and banners.

Other rooms—the various rooms in the student compound, the hospital where demonstration victims are brought, the book-filled apartment (with Shostakovich on the stereo) of the revisionist party bureaucrat—are echoes of the wedding room with its desire to close out history. They all replay the same attempt to substitute a space of personal values for history's expansiveness. Take, for example, the hospital. Here, refusing to leave her bed to go back to the demonstration, the wounded student, Reika, meets the journalist, Nozawa; it is their marriage that we see take place as the dominant ceremony of the film.

Moreover, the few places that might stand as exceptions to this closure find themselves quickly giving in to those forces that are out to crush dissidence and collapse history onto personality. For example, the student dining hall should be a place of free discussion for the students, but the kind of discussion that does occur there demonstrates the extent to which political investigation and struggle is being repressed by group pressure and party line.

The political intervention of the film, however, does not simply come from Oshima's attempt to show an articulated politics that could replace the fixities and blindnesses of revisionism and overestimation of the personal. Rather, this political intervention derives from the film's technique, which itself qualifies an ideology of closure and calls it into question. Thus, the camera movement neutralizes the wedding ceremony, revealing the extent to which a kind of political night and fog is actually present in the room. In other words, not only do the radicals break into the wedding to remind the guests of a history of struggle that they are denying by that very ceremony; the camera itself breaks in, as well. What some critics have attacked as theatrical effects in the film—the way, for example, that Oshima suddenly shifts from the wedding room to the outside where demonstrations occur—is in fact evidence of the power of the film's cinematic codes to encourage a kind of alienation effect.[2] The film is like the radical students in its story, refusing to do things according to established rules and proprieties. If *Night and Fog in Japan* is "theatrical," it is so precisely in the sense of Brecht's aesthetic: events are put inside quotation marks, spoken by an historical knowledge that is more committed and complete, and that is not simply a knowledge possessed by characters in the story. In Oshima's film, knowledge is passed between characters, aesthetic form, and the spectators.

In analyzing the ceremony of the marriage, *Night and Fog in Japan* also analyzes another ceremony: the act of filmgoing itself. This is not to suggest that the film breaks spectator pleasure; on the contrary, the film presupposes the use of the cinematic experience as a ceremony of personal pleasure in order to qualify and situate that pleasure. Specifically, the film exhibits a strong use of what Roland Barthes calls the hermeneutic code—why did Takao die? where did Kitami disappear to? how did the police spy escape?—in order to implicate the spectator in a structure of suspense that the film will subsequently interrogate.

Like, say, *Citizen Kane, Night and Fog in Japan* uses interlacing flashbacks to show how present actions are determined by past ones. Moreover, these flashbacks are assumed to stand in some way as answers to the engendering questions of the film. But *Night and Fog in Japan*'s answers are of a different order than that of the questions it starts with. Indeed, the answers are far different from those that the revisionist characters in the film come up with in order to avoid facing their political situation. The true answers to the questions must be politically aware. For example, why did Takao commit suicide? Because of dogmatic pressures from the party—pressures that the party members refuse to avow. In *Citizen Kane,* with its adherence to a particular (Oedipal) notion of biography, there is finally nothing improbable about a sled named Rosebud explaining the life of a man in a film that all along has not been so much about the citizen, Kane, as about the personality, Kane. By contrast, *Night and Fog in Japan* works to answer its questions in ways that the clichés of psychology cannot account for. As Sylvia Trosa suggests, "In the mingling of accounts, the characters end up by losing their individual importance in the face of the intricate tableau of a global situation, an historical and complex logic that they have not known how to master, not even how to catch a glimpse of, and that their words don't always discern" (review of *Night and Fog in Japan,* 1980).

In going beyond the individual(ist) explanations that each of the characters provides to justify the situation he/she is in, *Night and Fog in Japan* moves the spectator beyond those explanations; the spectator's identification is more with the camera itself than with any of the characters (and even figures like Ota the radical who brings politics into the personal represent only a limited form of political intervention). Whereas the hermeneutic code normally works to provide a resolution that, although perhaps unexpected, leads to the ultimate sense that the ending makes sense, *Night and Fog in Japan* gives its spectators a new set of answers—answers not apparent in the original posing of the enigma. The film works as a kind of teaching device to suggest to the spectator that any number of human practices must be understood as having their ultimate sense in the previously unthought-of realm of politics. Part of the project of the film's technique is to challenge that function of narrative as a conversion of difference into a logic of positioning that theorists like Stephen Heath see as part of the process of classical narrativity. For classical narrativity, the new is merely an extension of the already given. In contrast, *Night and Fog in Japan* suggests that an unexpected new way of thinking can break into an established logic with all the force of revolution. For example, when offscreen space becomes onscreen space through the movement of the camera, it is not an appropriation of the new by the old but, in direct contrast, a challenge to the complacency of the old by the new. Against the symmetry of the wedding that tries to deny history, the camera movement serves as a figure for the movement and changeability of historical reality; the first four minutes of the opening shot signal this tension, as the movement of the camera enters into conflict with the movement of one of the intruders *and* with the lateral movement of the titles across the screen, creating a play on positions of knowledge and politics.

The power of the camera to qualify and to relativize any composition, any position, may, however, limit the political power of the film; the camera itself becomes an authority figure, a source of knowledge that the spectator relies upon. The positioning of the camera as authority is never itself qualified, never criticized in a way that might lead the spectator to understand cinema itself as an historically situated force. *Night and Fog in Japan*'s questioning camerawork interrogates positions but, in doing no more than call into question every position but its own, the film may encourage a quietism, the sense that eternal questioning is all that is possible. Thus, the last shot invokes the repetitions of unhistorical thinking, and, in many ways, such an ending seems inevitable for the film. Ota, the Trotskyite, runs out into the fog and is arrested and taken away by the police. Some of the wedding guests rush off to organize a demonstration against his arrest, but most remain behind in immobility listening to the revisionist, Nakayama, drone on and on about the need for moderation. The camera circles around and around this immobility, ultimately finding rest only in the fog from which it originated. Having discredited every political position and each one's claim to completeness, the camera can rest nowhere except in the nothingness of the non-place of the fog. Significantly absent from *Night and Fog in Japan* is any mediation of, any distance from, the cinematic project itself. It is in fact such a distance that might well establish an advance over the limitations of positions in and of the film; the one position that can go beyond the characters and, more than that, beyond the work of the film, is the position of the spectator. While the camera movement and film techniques can serve as a figuration of political issues—relating, comparing, criticizing various political positions—a self-reflexivity might work to move the experience of film beyond that of a watching of preestablished figures to a production of not yet existent situations.

The importance of Oshima's *Death by Hanging* derives from its attention to structures of cinematic authority. The film plays out this attention as an interaction between a politics of figuration like that in *Night and Fog in Japan* and a distance instituted between spectator and figure. The structure of the film is again one of repetition: the hanging at the end of the film repeats the hanging at the beginning in which R's body had refused to die. But the repetition is not perfect. When the hangman's rope falls through the trapdoor during the final hanging, R disappears and an empty noose dangles. Thematically, the empty noose can signify the emptiness of judicial processes. But the image is more than a signifier for processes within the story of the film; it is also the concluding moment to a process of implication of the spectator into the movement of the film.

The opening sequence of the film fixes the spectator in a position of complacency as a mere observer of an event that he/she presumes to understand and find relatively unproblematic. The sequence, which is shot to look like a documentary, promises to show by means of a real hanging the efficient workings of the judicial system. That is, the documentary style converts hanging from a political act into a merely technical one; thus, we learn minor details about the various switches and buttons that open the trap door. Then, too, the official point of view of the witnesses matches ours perfectly, overdetermining the viewing situation as a particularly safe one. But there suddenly appears this title: "the body of the prisoner R refuses to die." Intruding into the secure space of the hanging ceremony, this title forcefully questions the values and suppositions that the film spectators and the characters in the witness box hold in regard to that ceremony. In this sense, it seems not so unlike the emergence of the radicals out of the fog in *Night and Fog in Japan.* But the spectator's previous identification with a point of view in the film—that of the officials at the hanging—allows for a subsequent disturbing of identification that was not as possible in *Night and Fog in Japan,* where the spectator exists outside all positions in the film from the very first moment. In *Death by Hanging,* a certain identification between spectator and attitudes in the film is encouraged, all the better for the film to then proceed on its course of distantiation. Indeed, as I suggested in my discussion of Brechtian aesthetics, the aesthetics of distantiation would seem to rest on the notion of an initial positing of values (those that the spectator brings in from outside the theater, those that he/she upholds as values in everyday life) which the aesthetic project then relativizes. Distantiation always works from a previously held position of identification. In each invocation of cultural value, *Death by Hanging* seems to endorse that value to then suggest the political assumptions that uphold values and that are normally repressed in order to let values function: for example, to assume that a murderer is guilty for his/her crime may be to ignore the social forces that can encourage and lead to crime.

Like the earlier film, *Death by Hanging* plays on codes of inside and outside; here again, the inside is figured as the space of containment. Most notably, the officials construct a number of sets inside the execution room so that R can replay his past, accept his identity, and so once again be the reified subject of legal discourse and practice. Similarly, the outside represents the challenge of historicity to the secure world of containment. Thus, in remembering his past, R brings to the sketches that the officials have concocted for him knowledge and values that can only upset the reifying goals of those sketches. When the officials ask R to replay his crimes so that he will accept what they see as his legal responsibility, the replaying leads to facts about the crimes (for example, that they were political in origin, bearing a fundamental relationship to the Japanese oppression of Korea) that the officials had ignored or repressed.

Fundamentally, though, the codes of identification are played on in *Death by Hanging* in a way that they are not in *Night and Fog in Japan*. Because *Death by Hanging* so immediately plays on the spectator's faith in certain generic codings (for example, the visual look of a documentary), the distance that the spectator finally takes is a distance not only from the narrative meanings in the film but also from the values that comprise the act of film viewing itself. That is, when the officials in the story come to realize that knowing an individual is no simple activity (or is simple only at the price of a reduction, a distorting capture of the individual within cultural stereotypes), the spectator similarly comes to the realization that knowing a film is a simple activity only when the film corresponds to dominant generic classifications or stereotypes. By showing how a few stylistic traits, such as "authoritative" narration, can all too easily make us watch as a documentary what is actually a fiction, *Death by Hanging* upsets our faith in our standard classifications.

Realm of the Senses, a hard-core film in which "everything is shown," might well seem an abandonment of the critique of story and identification that characterizes a film like *Death by Hanging*. Indeed, *Realm* seems initially easy to read, its usually unmoving camera impassively registering the sexual acts before it (and even sometimes increasing the visibility of these acts as in the three shots that move from long shot to close-up the first time that Sada performs fellatio on Kichi).

Finding a political engagement with form in the ways that the film's cutting violates set rules of editing, Stephen Heath, in his essay "The Question Oshima," argues that *Realm of the Senses* is of fundamental importance for the ways that it can challenge the voyeurism of cinematic spectacle by editing patterns that refuse to uphold conventions of screen space construction. For example, the opening shots that concentrate on images of Sada looking are only partially sutured by shots of the target of her look. And yet, the brute presence of the sex, its unquestionable hereness, can repress attention to and recognition of any play at the level of form. In the opening scene, the few glimpses that we do get of the sexual activity that Sada is looking at tend to become the predominant interest of the scene, as one explicit moment in a film that, by reputation, promises many more such moments. Antivoyeuristic on the level of its formal articulations, *Realm of the Senses* can seem to recuperate voyeurism on the level of the cultural resonances attached to sexual imagery.[3]

Indeed, in its representation of a certain kind of repetition (sexual acts that lead to death), *Realm of the Senses* would appear to be a regression from the critique of the ahistorical, of the nondialectical modes of thinking, employed in *Death by Hanging* and *Night and Fog in Japan*. The film's story is virtually a literalization of Freud's understanding in *Beyond the Pleasure Principle* of the death instinct as a repetitive insistence that eventually draws even the pleasure principle under its sway. The three attempts (the final one successful) by Sada to strangle Kichi during their lovemaking are so many attempts to bring to completion a process that seems inevitably built into their relationship from the start. The inescapability of this repetitive encounter with death works as a structuring force in the film as, for example, in the repeated visual citation of the knife that Sada is trying to use against another woman when she (Sada) first meets Kichi, and that is like the one with which she will finally castrate Kichi. These repetitions work all the more to move the action of the film into a personal realm: Kichi and Sada retreat from contact with an outside world into the personal sphere of their own obsessions where there is no room for the third person, the social Other. As if to confirm the personal nature of Sada's and Kichi's story, the film includes three fantasy sequences, all of which are clearly assigned to Sada; this enclosing of vision, of imagining, within the viewpoint of particular characters is very different from the role of fantasy in *Death by Hanging* where the fantasy (that a hanged man's body could live on even if his soul had died) is not attributed to any character alone but is the enabling condition for the film's whole operation on its spectators.

In his essay, Heath, quoting with approval Lacan's declaration that "the limit of history is death," argues that, beyond formal complexity, it may well be in the repetitive engagement with death that *Realm of the Senses* finds the source for a political engagement. Heath's argument here is the poststructuralist one in which textual inscriptions of the death instinct are valorized as refusals, excesses, of the text.[4] For this approach, all practices exist in relation to an inevitable drive toward death, but it is the bad faith of representation to deny this, to repress death as an otherness, an outside. In Heath's words, "that connection [between sex and death] is known in classic cinema but exactly as the violence and dispersion which apparatus and narrative are there to contain . . . " ("The Question Oshima," p. 81). Where a film like *Meet Me in St. Louis* will confine death to a number of sharply demarcated and contained scenes (for example, the Halloween night sequence),[5] *Realm of the Senses* unrepresses the repressed; for Heath, the shock-value of the film lies in the showing not of sex but of death, that "fading of the text" (as he puts it, paraphrasing Lacan) in which story and the representation together realize loss. Whereas the pleasure principle, in the practice of classic narrative, has become fundamentally adaptive, hiding the loss of the human subject beneath the plenitude of specular fullness, death is subversive, its textualization bringing about a deconstruction of selfhood.

To an extent, Oshima's own declarations approve of such a reading. Oshima's defense comments at his obscenity trial argue that the film celebrates the ends, even fatal ones, to which free sexuality will go in order to reject constraining definitions of the sexual and the social:

> The sexual morality of Christianity, which only authorizes the sexual act insofar as the man and the woman, who have made a covenant before God, a unique God, practice it to the exclusive ends of procreation, was a morality that particularly fitted in well with the Japanese State in the Meiji era. . . . Such a love as Sada's and Kichi's could be born only between beings who shared the idea that the human being, including his/her sexual being, is originally completely free and that everything is permitted. . . . In an epoch when Japanese men were being mobilized to die on the fields of battle, there was this man, Ishida Kichizo, who died with joy in order to satisfy the love and sexuality of a woman." ("Plaidoyer," pp. 10-11)

Oshima seems to recognize, though, the inadequacy of such a position: "I employ the word 'sadness" to describe the liberatory attitude because the fact that the human being is completely, totally free and that everything is permitted him/her is extremely terrifying" (ibid., p. 12). In fact, I think we can find in *Realm of the Senses* a practice of film that calls into question the obsession with the personal and with death and with the "liberatory" possibility of sexuality per se. This practice is a repetitive intrusion, running against the repetition of death, of the outside world into the inner space of the personal—an intrusion that serves as a reminder of the weight and unavoidability of historical time.

The title of the film literally translates as *Corrida of Love;* Sada and Kichi's story is, indeed, like the bullfight, a ritual encounter with death (to the point of one of the participant's severing and carrying with pride one of the body parts of the other). The inwardness of Sada and Kichi's relationship is so obsessive that it turns all locales into sites for their sexual ceremony; indeed, at one point, when they have taken a room in an inn, Kichi says to Sada, "We are not in town, we are still at home." Quite simply, the lovers can turn any location—a rickshaw, a porch, steps—into a corrida, with red (as in Sada's kimono) serving as an ever-present reminder of the ceremonial qualities of their actions. The film repeats the concern with ceremonies, with a ritual process supposedly outside the sway of everyday cares, that Oshima's other films exhibit. And, like the other films, this ritual process is constantly intruded into, exceeded, by the responsibilities and demands of the social world. To be sure, Oshima's own comments on the film tend to read Sada and Kichi's activities as a testament to essential drives of life and death in a world that is socially constricting. But at the same time, and in a way that is offered up for the viewer's potential observation and criticism, *Realm of the Senses* specifies the losses and constrictions that can result from a too-strong concentration on the personal, on the retreat into the self or the autonomous couple. Sada and Kichi may be rebels, but their rebellion is of a particularly limited and self-destructive kind. Significantly, their adventures takes place in 1936, on the eve of a military takeover in Japan—a takeover that was to spell the end of the very kind of life that Sada and Kichi led.

The narrative of *Realm of the Senses*—a pair of lovers alienated from the outside world—and its echo in the style of the film—the disjunctive editing, the play with and against suturing that Stephen Heath notes—closely approximate the kind of textualization of alienation that Fredric Jameson in his *Fables of Aggression: Wyndham Lewis, the Modernist as Fascist* (1979) sees figured in modernist art. What *Realm of the Senses* enacts is a kind of dissociation in the heart of the social world, a dissociation that shows up as an aggressivity toward the Other (in Lewis's case, modern mass culture; in *Realm,* the sexual prudence of Showa Japan). Ultimately, this aggressivity turns inward to affect its agents: thus, in killing Kichi, Sada only incompletely realizes that Bataillan quest for a merging of pleasure and pain—she has also killed part of herself, as we see when, right after Kichi's death, a fantasy scene from Sada's point of view shows her alone among endless rows of wooden benches as she plaintively calls out for Kichi.

Jameson suggests that a recurrent figurative pattern in modernist narrative is the pseudo-couple. Against an outside world pictured as a threat to self, individuals will form enclaves in which a liberation of values is supposed to occur, but where, more often, the very antagonisms, repressions, violations of the outside world of sociality intrude and are replayed on a one-on-one scale. Sada and Kichi are a pseudo-couple in this sense. Far from a relationship of love, theirs is an alienated relationship (Sada, remember, is a prostitute with assigned social functions) in which contact and interaction with the other is reduced metonymically to contact with little more than the sex of the other. Oshima's visual composition helps to underscore this fact. For example, the first time that Sada fellates Kichi, the composition arranges Kichi's body across the long horizontal of the screen, his genital region at one side, and the upper part of his body way at the other side where he lifts a cigarette to his mouth and impassively smokes it.

The moments when Sada and Kichi communicate with each other in any way other than the sexual are rare in the course of the film. Late in the story, when Kichi remarks that in making love to an old woman he felt as if he had been making love to his mother, this occasions a discussion between Sada and Kichi about their past life. This appears to be the first time that they have had to talk to each other about who they are. Indeed, the concentration of each on the genitals of the other occurs to the detriment of the whole personality, since Sada and Kichi have never really had full personalities to present to each other. When we first see them, Sada and Kichi are so tightly bound to their social roles that their subsequent obsession with sex becomes little more than a substitution of one fixity for another.

This alienation in the relationship, then, is an echoing of a more general alienation between all the characters in the film, especially as they interact with the pseudo-couple of Sada and Kichi. The attitude of the outside world begins as either disdain or a kind of passive fascination that can easily find itself drawn into an involvement more than tinged with a kind of destructiveness. For example, at Sada and Kichi's mock wedding, a curious onlooker is violated with a piece of carved wood by other geishas. The attitude of the pseudo-couple toward the outside world is likewise either one of mediation through a reduction of that world to one of sexual desire alone (as when Sada instantly offers her body in exchange for drinks at a bar that has closed for the night) or one of aggression (twice, Sada tries to encourage Kichi to rape women).

In all this figuration of alienation, *Realm of the Senses* would seem initially to be a critique of obsession only in that sense in which Jameson sees Lewis's fascist texts to be a critique of fascism; that is, an unintentional self-critique that occurs only because the text follows to its excessive conclusions and thus lays bare a number of premises that it would have been safer for it to conceal beneath the proprieties of secondary revision. But it is possible, I would suggest, to read *Realm of the Senses* as a critique that operates through a distance that it appears to take from the fragmented and obsessive world of the film's story. Most importantly, it is through the intervention of the spectator who exists apart from the story that *Realm of the Senses* engages in its critique.

In the way that it attempts to deny the outside world or to mold it to its own obsessions, Sada and Kichi's relationship is doomed to the failure of any kind of relationship that tries simply to remove itself from the social context.[6] Most immediately, their relationship runs up against the limits imposed by social scarcity—the need, for example, to work to support the private realm (thus, in one scene, Sada has to go back to a client). Significantly, as soon as Sada and Kichi admit this one social need, the closures of their relationship crack open. For example, when Sada leaves the second time to sleep with her client, maids come and clean out the room in which she and Kichi had tried to create their private space.

Significantly, *Realm of the Senses* encourages a critique of the lovers' relationship by appealing to the spectator's superiority of knowledge over that of the characters. In this regard, a very subtle signifier occurs in the film at the level of composition and color scheme: a great number of shots have a red object—sometimes a kimono, sometimes the rose color of a body—in the center of the frame surrounded by a field of whiteness. Here, what on the level of representation is no more than an index of the object filmed becomes for an interpreting spectator a sign whose meaning must be decoded. For example, the image can become a representation at the level of style of a signification that had already been explicitly present in the film's story. Hence, the red and white of the Japanese flag (like the one that young children brandish in the second scene of the film); the omnipresence of bloody death and violence (for example, the last shot of Kichi's body, the red of blood against his pale corpse); the insistent omnipresence of genital sexuality (the redness or pinkness of the male or female sex organs against the lightness of the body); and finally, a reference to the corrida and to all ceremonies (like that of Japanese militarism) that all too often end in death. The film works according to such resonances, such critical and intellectual repetitions whose interconnections are the task of the spectator; performing this task, the spectator can engage in a transcendence of the initial premises of the film.

Frequently, the film gives the spectator information that the characters do not possess. A strong example of this occurs when Sada goes for the second time to visit her client and Kichi goes out to get a haircut. There is a close-up of Kichi wrapped up in his thoughts as he leaves the barbershop. But, as Kichi continues down a street in long shot, soldiers come marching up the street past him. Although short in duration and seemingly extraneous, the scene takes up three shots (in a film that tends to be very sparing in its editing). The film returns to a close-up of Kichi, but the close-up is now different: it is no longer just a shot of a man alone with his thoughts. Rather, the sound of the marching soldiers continues offscreen, and, as they pass Kichi, they cause the pink light of the sun to play across his face. Kichi does not notice the soldiers—he has brought his obsessions along with him into the external world, so he misses a way potentially to understand the imbrication of the personal and the political (it was this military uprising that closed down Edo, the geisha and artisan part of Tokyo in 1936). But the spectator has a chance to make the connection, and with it to gain an understanding that is not available to Sada and Kichi, rooted as they are in their finished, fated historicity.

Realm of the Senses is not anywhere near the perfect political film (whatever that might be); in part, the punctuation of the obsessive by politics, by the awareness of sociality in all its force, is too infrequent and too weakly articulated to draw out a fully and politically dialogical interaction on the part of the spectator (thus, my comments on the film have to remain on the level of *an* interpretation). As intrusions of a *social* history, these moments are perhaps too elusive, requiring special knowledge and special ways of seeing that much of the subject of the film would seek to discourage. But the film suggests directions, carries on an engagement with the politics of the personal, that make it an important and challenging film.

Running through the whole of this study has been an argument about the politics of repetition—an argument that culminates in the discussion of certain films of Oshima as constituting a contribution to a cinema in which a history intrudes again and again into spaces that would like to forget that they are bound to the vagaries of history. This sort of cinematic repetition can stand in marked contrast to the sort of repetition employed in classic narrativity. This latter repetition involves the containment of the new by the old; difference, development, narrative change, are all functions generated and controlled by the initial terms of the text and so, in the long run, no *different* at all.

I have chosen to end with a discussion, however tentative, of some films directed by Nagisa Oshima because I find in these films the possibility of a new form of repetition: Oshima's repetition is an intrusion into the secure world of contained ideologies by a different set of values, ones that are questioning and criticizing. *Night and Fog in Japan,* for example, criticizes the present for the sake of a future (that exists not in the film but in the world of the spectator) by a recourse to the past as a rhetorical figure; the flashbacks, which belie the serenity of the diegetic present, insistently and repetitively demand that the spectator examine his/her own present to analyze what it represses so that he/she can go beyond that repression.

In *Différence et répétition* (1968), Gilles Deleuze compares "complex" repetition (as against a repetition that is caught in "identity, resemblance, analogy") to the dramatic activity of modern theater. His explicit reference is to Artaud's theater of cruelty where spectators don't merely see acts of drama but make those acts of drama themselves, through participation. While Deleuze's reference to Artaud's incantatory theater partakes strongly of an ideology of art as intuition and sentiment,[7] his sense of complex repetition as a dramatization not so much of issues that spectators view but of the existence of those spectators themselves is close in form to the conception of productive repetition that I have tried to argue for here. Indeed, to echo my opening, Deleuze sees Marx, in "The Eighteenth Brumaire," as a central contributor to this way of thinking of drama as a movement beyond representation, a movement in which what is repeated is the future as a challenge to current ideological closures. For Deleuze, "When Marx criticizes the abstract and false movement or mediation of the Hegelians, he approaches an idea—that he indicates more than he develops—an idea that is essentially 'theatrical': insofar as history is a theatre, repetition, the tragic and the comic in repetition form a condition of movement, in which the 'actors' or 'heroes' produce something *effectively new* in history" (p. 19, my emphasis). A film like *Realm of the Senses* approaches this sense of production in the ways it puts its actors into the spectator's field of interrogation. The film demonstrates that the real actors of a film are not characters in the film, but the viewers who live in a real world where they can act and produce. Compared to a mythic utopian language of the future, Oshima's ambiguities may still be the stutterings of the infant that Marx sees in any break from the past. But Oshima's cinema still seems to be one of the few cinemas that dramatizes a repeated concern with the dialectics of screen and spectator.[8] In a way that is both different from but indebted to Stephen Heath's, I would suggest that what Heath calls "the Question Oshima" is one well worth addressing.

Appendix

Oshima Film Plots

Night and Fog in Japan

Reika and Nozawa, two former members of the Japanese left, are about to be married. They met when Reika was hospitalized during a demonstration, and their marriage signals a desire to put the radicalism of the past behind them. But Ota and Takumi, fervent participants in ongoing struggles, break into the wedding ceremony. The intrusion causes the wedding participants and guests to remember and review their past involvement in the left. Much of the current desire is to forget one particular incident in which a captured rightist was accidentally freed by a young radical named Takao who later committed suicide because of party pressure. Having stirred up memories, Ota finally leaves the wedding but is immediately arrested by the police. Once again, the characters in the story react in various ways, from the ineffectual speech-making of the revisionist, Nakayama, to the voluntarist attempts at immediate struggle by a number of young radicals who rush off, with no clear plans, to intervene for Ota.

Death by Hanging

The Korean immigrant, R, is being executed for the rape-murder of a Japanese girl. But while R's soul dies, his body refuses to follow suit. The Japanese officials decide that their only option is to treat R as a *tabula rasa* who must be reeducated to adopt his full identity. However, as this reeducation proceeds, the officials uncover more of the mediations which govern Korea's subordinate position to Japan, and which have made R what he is, than the officials would like to have known about. For example, the woman the officials employ in a recreation of the crime turns into a radical Korean who refuses her Japan-imposed social role and implores R to maintain his integrity as a Korean. When R finally agrees that he is R, the officials recommence the hanging. But R is now no longer the simple, controllable object that the officials' original practice had assumed him to be. When the noose drops through the trapdoor, it is empty.

Realm of the Senses

Based on an actual event, *Realm* chronicles the love affair between a maid in a geisha house and the husband of the house's director. Kichi and Sada find that their love-making requires doses of violence and pain to keep it exciting. Finally, in a paroxysm of passion, Sada strangles Kichi and castrates him. A voice-over explains that this happened in 1936.

Notes

Chapter 1

1. For purposes of convenience, the footnoting in this study strikes a compromise between end-notes and parenthetical citations in the text. References to cited texts will be given in abbreviated form in the body of the work; full bibliographic information for all citations may be found in the bibliography. End-notes will be reserved for discussions or clarifications of material in the text.

2. If Eisenstein's approach is a rejection of the reflectionist, superstructural model (art shows the real but is in a subordinate relation to it), it also rejects the opposite model, that of art as that which is outside the social and which is no more than a context-free play of forms. This model, most represented by poststructuralism with its emphasis on a freeing of signifiers from any communicative end, is a dominant ideology in contemporary investigations of aesthetic politics; using the critiques of formalism in Eisenstein's or Brecht's realism, I hope to suggest the possibilities for a critique of today's formalism.

3. This is the polemical reading, for example, of Marx's concept of "pre-capitalist modes of production" which Barry Hindess and Paul Q. Hirst argue for in their *Pre-Capitalist Modes of Production*. Hindess and Hirst suggest that Marx uses such a concept not so much because of its supposed real existence (even though such may have been Marx's *conscious* intent) but rather because of its structural necessity in the fabric of Marx's argument and its logic. (See Hindess and Hirst, 1975). For applications and criticism of this position in film historiography, see the collection of the 1977 Edinburgh Film Festival, *History/Production/Memory* (Claire Johnson, ed., 1977).

4. This is to argue against, for example, the poetic analysis of Marx which Hayden White provides in his *Metahistory: The Historical Imagination in 19th Century Europe* (White, 1973). White's analysis of the ways history writing phantasmically figures the past provides a useful typology—a *combinatoire*—of the strategies of historiography (although White's text needs the same kind of analysis as a useful fiction itself). But White's view of history writing as an epistemological act—that is, an observation from *outside* history of what is going on *inside*—can give no place to the material effectivity of history writing as productive act, to the ways writing has an effect on its readers.

5. However, as I will show in my discussion of Brecht, this detour is no less political. Theater for Brecht is not only a presentation of social activity, but a social activity itself. Brecht's aesthetic is not so much an intervention in content but in the ways content is presented and the *effects* different presentations can have.

6. A good critique of cinematic essentialism is the opening chapter, "What Isn't Cinema?," in Gerald Mast's *Film/Cinema/Movie*, 1977. Mast suggests how aesthetic theories usually extend a valorization of one kind of film to cinema in general, with a resultant distortion of what cinema is. Unfortunately, Mast's own subsequent attempt to create a general theory of film falls into an essentialism of its own: *all* films, he argues, are kinetic or mimetic in function. (For a critique of essentialist theories of film, and Mast's own inability to escape this idealist problematic, see my review of *Film/Cinema/Movie* in *The Journal of Aesthetics and Art Criticism,* 1977).

7. For the discussion of specific codes, see Metz's *Langage et Cinéma,* 1971. Specific codes are the signifying practices specific to a particular type of communication (for example, editing is specific to film and television although it can be approximated in other arts as in the "montage" sequence in *Madame Bovary*).

8. A useful introduction to the concept of "specific signifying practice" is Stephen Heath's "*Jaws,* Ideology, and Film Theory," *Film Reader* 2, 1977.

9. See Bellour, "The Unattainable Text," 1975. My use of "unattainable" here is different from Bellour's, though. For Bellour, film is in particular unattainable because its inexorable flow through a projector makes it hard for the analyst to fully grasp its meaning (and, further, because its specific materiality makes it hard for the analyst to quote it in his/her analysis, his/her re-writing); Bellour's use of motion-analyzing equipment, his concern for close reading, are attempts to attain the film, to make it a graspable text like all others. My argument is that all texts in whatever area of discourse (writing as well as film) are unattainable to the extent that what analytic knowledge can only know is not a practice but a mere reification, a simulacrum, of practice.

10. See Enzensberger, "The Consciousness Industry" in his book of the same title (1974). See also Armand Mattelart's critique of the notion that dominant culture is a "conscious Frankenstein" in his "The Nature of Communication Practices in a Dependent Society," 1978.

11. In his discussion of Ealing Studio films, John Ellis's point about proffered codes is precisely that this proffering was not necessarily accepted; there was a schism between the middle-class world view of the Ealing filmmakers and their lower-class audiences. See Ellis, "Made in Ealing" (1975).

    On the concept of leakage and its implications for art, see Richard Dyer, *Stars* (1979), p. 28: discussing debates as to whether certain acting roles are ultimately recuperative or subversive of a dominant ideology, Dyer asks, "how . . . can one actually distinguish with any rigour between the two? . . . The answer to that depends on how hermetic your conception of the mass media, and of ideology, is. My own belief is that the system is a good deal more 'leaky' than many people would currently maintain. . . . "

12. See the chapter on *S/Z* in Coward and Ellis, *Language and Materialism* (1977) for a useful discussion of this hierarchy of the codes.

13. Interestingly, Simon accuses content analysis of contextualism—"analysis of the film vanishes in the face of reference to the context, a positivistic reduction of text to context" (ibid.)—as if understanding, interpretation, were ever anything but application of a context. Against the indeterminacy of content, Simon shifts attention to formal structures. In this lies the source of his formalism: the assumption that certain forms have a permanent and direct tie to certain meanings just waiting for the critic to discover them.

    A useful critique of the notion that there is one method that grants the interpreter a direct, context-free access to the meaning of a text is Walter Benn Michaels, "Against Formalism: the Autonomous Text in Legal and Literary Interpretation" (1979). Using the example of legal interpretation, Michaels suggests that formalist interpretation is an attempt to diminish ambiguity by measuring the less stable (a form) to the more stable (the meaning that is ostensibly always an attribute of that form). But, as Michaels argues, it is a myth that there is a stable core of meaning behind any form; the context in which that form makes its meaning has a shaping force on that meaning. For a similar critique of the myth of stability in formalism, see the critique of "dictionary meaning" (that is, of a fixed index of meanings) which runs though V.N. Voloshinov, *Marxism and the Philosophy of Language* (1973).

14.   For a useful introduction to the problem of formalism as political intervention specifically as it is argued out in Burch's work, see the debate on Burch in *Jump Cut* 10/11 with articles by Chuck Kleinhans, "Swinging on Burch's Theory," and Martin Walsh, "Noel Burch's Film Theory."

15.   This position comes from early premises of Russian formalism: the history of form is fundamentally its formal history, and its relation to other historical series is one of parallelism rather than integration or mediation.

16.   "The people who most need to study this [Japanese] cinema in its most 'radically Japanese' form are those committed to constructing a thorough-going critique of the dominant modes of Western cinema" (p. 17).

17.   This in a writer who admits he doesn't know Japanese very well and relies on authoritative texts for his historical information. Burch even goes so far as to see his inability to understand spoken Japanese as an advantage since it ostensibly allows him to concentrate on formal aspects of "modes of representation." Yet speech is not just an aspect of content but also part of its formal structure; even the most seemingly classical, representational Hollywood film would gain in formal complexity if one didn't understand English.

18.   As recent feminist critiques of the use of "woman" as an Other have suggested, there is also something imperialist about any appeal to a particular social group (in Burch's case, the Japanese) as fundamentally critical of another group: the consequence is to essentialize Otherness, to give the critical group no effect other than a virtually magical one as outsider. This is to rob social forces of the multiplicity of their interventions in history.

19.   From the start, Burch's approach is fundamentally opposed to any attempt to capture experiences of films by spectators in real situations. The use of motion-analyzing equipment does not explain the films that audiences have seen but literally *creates new films.*

20.   See, for example, the discussion of the duplicitous text, of the lying flashback, in Kristin Thompson's "The Duplicitous Text: An Analysis of *Stage Fright*," *Film Reader* (1977).

21.   The classic presentation of a hierarchy of the ways films "are" political is Jean-Louis Comolli's and Jean Narboni's "Cinema/Ideology/Criticism" (reprinted in *Movies and Methods*, 1976).

22.   On the question of codical displacement and the imbrication of specific/nonspecific codes, see Metz, *Langage et cinéma* (1971).

23.   It is in this fact that Burch's aforementioned problem with the soundtrack (note 17) has its source. Burch categorically puts sound on the side of content and so condemns its expressive use in film.

24.   This is not at all to suggest that this study will not present, or even valorize, a tradition of its own. However, my argument is that most theories of film are formalist in their attention to a practice contained in the film, in the film as sole source of meaning. I will suggest that a different practice of film, one which treats the film itself as only one source among many, is possible and that roots of such a practice can be located in certain exemplary film practices.

25. Research on feminine masochism has shown the multiple effects and functions—both positive and negative—of social practices beyond any simple fact of wish fulfillment. See, for example, the analyses of women's popular culture by Tania Modleski, *Loving with a Vengeance* (1982).

26. See, for example, Kristeva's binary opposition of semiotic and semantic which is precisely a distinction along these lines.

27. Derrida's displacement of the nature of Western practice from one of rationality to one of presence (which incorporates rationality as *one* of its modalities) does little to alter the problem. In the identification of the West as based on a metaphysics of presence, there is the tautology that people accept the reassurance of the metaphysical tradition because it is reassuring because it is metaphysical. Contradiction (for example, the various motivations behind the desire for a presence; the various forms in which reassurance can occur; the positive aspects of utopian thought) give way to a dichotomy of *construction,* the monolith of system, and *deconstruction,* the multitude of practices of *bricolage,* with no area for contradiction between them.

28. On the ways media forms function to resolve lower order contradictions, only to generate or be caught up in new contradiction, see Stuart Ewen, *Captains of Consciousness: Advertising and the Social Roots of the Consumer Culture* (1977).

29. For the first argument, see Ian Watt, *The Rise of the Novel* (1957); for the second, see Raymond Williams, "A Lecture on Realism," *Screen* (1972).

30. This is not to suggest, though, that there is any fixed connection between the rational and the manifest on the one hand, and the irrational and the latent on the other.

31. See "What's at Stake in the Woman's Struggle," *Sub-Stance* (1978). However, in other work, Lyotard also falls into an essentializing argument; see my comments below on his essay, "Acinema."

32. The discussion here of Baudrillard is based on two texts, *Pour une critique de l'économie politique du signe* (1972) and *Le miroir de la production* (1973).

33. A problem in Baudrillard is his tendency (although it is no more than that) to see political control as conspiratorial and intentional; this seems implicit in his reference to "strategies." Significantly, as an inverse corollary, Baudrillard is unable to envision any form of struggle, positive or negative, against sign-production; there is still a recourse to manipulation theory in his work.

34. For example, see Pierre Macherey, "The Problem of Reflection," *Sub-Stance* (1978).

35. For Althusser on ideology and art, see "Ideology and Ideological State Apparati," and "A Letter on Art in Reply to André Daspre," both in *Lenin and Philosophy* (1971).

36. For the spatial representation of this placing of art, see Terry Eagleton, *Criticism and Ideology* (1976), p. 80.

37. See, especially, the essay, "Fonction-signe et logique de classe" in *Pour une critique.*

38. For a critique of the notion that it is only in narrative that the representational containment of women occurs, see Laura Mulvey, "Narrative Cinema and Visual Pleasure," *Screen* (1975). Mulvey's essay analyzes a number of different ways in which narrative and image can interact in representation.

39. See "Articulations of the Cinematic Code" (reprinted in *Movies and Methods*) and *A Theory of Semiotics* (1973a).

40. For Macherey, see *Pour une théorie de la production littéraire* (1966); for Marcuse, see *The Aesthetic Dimension* (1978).

41. On this shift, see the introduction to *Screen's* "Metz and Semiotics" issue and Metz's own critique of Mitry's phenomenology in that issue (1974).

42. This is not to set up a before/after understanding with an originary myth on the one side and its subsequent expression in various forms on the other. A myth never exists outside its expressions, but the political space for the myth does.

43. This is not at all to attribute any final political meaning or effect to such disturbances of a myth; one can reject one myth all the better to confirm another. For example, the *Playgirl* kind of representation of men may reject the myth that only women are objects only to confirm another social myth: that what really defines *all* people is physical beauty.

44. For a presentation of this argument, see Lee Russell (pseudonym for Peter Wollen), "Sam Fuller," *New Left Review* (1964).

45. As my earlier discussion of the inadequacy of form/content distinctions suggested, the distinction between history in the text and the text in history is not always a sharp, definable one. To incorporate a new political content in an artwork may also be to incorporate that work itself into its political context differently.

Chapter 2

1. See, for example, the introduction by Naoum Kleiman, curator of the Eisenstein archives, to Eisenstein, *Esquisses et dessins* (1978).

2. But for a critique of the way in which *Cahiers du Cinéma* engaged in its rediscovery project, see Marcelin Pleynet, "The Left Front in Art: Eisenstein and the Young Hegelians" (*Screen Reader,* 1977).

3. Stalin, paradoxically, seems to be one of the few Soviet officials to have not lost admiration for Eisenstein (which may explain how Eisenstein escaped any of the possible fates that many of his comrades fell prey to). On the place of Eisenstein in Stalinist Russia, see the suggestive article by Kristin Thompson, "Ivan the Terrible and Stalinist Russia: A Reexamination" (*Cinema Journal,* 1977).

4. Pierre Sorlin's and Marie-Claire Ropars's analyses of the opening sequence of *October (Octobre: Ecriture et Idéologie,* 1976)—in which a heavily edited sequence shows the dismantling of a statue of the Tzar—suggests one reading of the complicated montage patterns of the sequence that approximates the definition of realism not as a transparent reflection of a real, but as a work of production. Ropars's analysis, for example, reads the sequence as a narrative of an increasing abstraction or transcendence of the actual (the pre-Soviet world). The opening shots show a statue of the Tzar—in fact, these images virtually build up the statue from fragments—and then localize the statue by a close-up of a descriptive plaque at its base. But almost immediately, the scene shifts to images of mobility (crowds running, rifles raised in anger, ropes thrown over the statue) which lead finally to a kind of deconstruction (Ropars's word) of the statue both in the narrative and in the filmic *écriture.* Ropars argues that it is only by shifting to a different register—by rejecting the brute facticity, the here-and-now of the statue in the initial shots—that the subjects of the film, the film itself, and the audience can move beyond the political givens of pre-Soviet Russia.

5. Two volumes of Bazin's general writings are available in English under the title *What is Cinema?* For a useful introduction to Bazin, see Dudley Andrew, *André Bazin* (1978).

6. It is this idea that Metz borrows directly from Bazin to form the notion of film as a *parole* without a *langue*. For a critique of the Bazinian tradition of semiotics of cinema, see the final chapter, "Semiology of the Cinema," in Peter Wollen's *Signs and Meanings in the Cinema* (1972).

7. For a discussion of Bazin's conception of the evolution of film language *as a language*, see Peter Wollen, "Ontology and Materialism in Film" (*Screen*, 1976).

8. Godard's argument in *La Chinoise*—that this history should be reversed to see Melies as film's first documentarian, and Lumière as the last of the great impressionists—is no mere flippancy. It is articulated as an attack on the narrowness of the Bazinian definition of reality.

9. The translation is Aumont's in *Montage Eisenstein*. For discussion of the reasons for such a translation, see pp. 181-82 in Aumont.

10. Bazin and Eisenstein move even closer together when seen in the light of Russian formalist and structuralist investigations into realism as a particular coded system (see, for example, Roman Jakobson's "On Realism in Art" in Matejka and Pomorska, *Readings in Russian Poetics,* 1971). For the formalists, realism is no more than *an* aesthetic—that is, a particular coded system that articulates itself as a set of conventions and conventional devices. Indeed, a critique of Bazin has been initiated precisely along these lines; he has been criticized for idealistically seeing a universal nature (i.e., truth) where there is in fact no more than a conventionalized cultural system. The realism that Bazin sees as a truly democratic art (democratic since, insofar as all of nature was declared to be meaningful, the viewer's attention would not need to be directed) is in fact *determined* at every moment. See Umberto Eco, "Articulations of the Cinematic Code" for the general outlines of the attack, and Jean-Louis Comolli, "Idéologie et technique" (*Cahiers du Cinéma*, 1971) for a close reading of Bazin's presuppositions. For example, Comolli analyzes shots from *Citizen Kane* (a central film in Bazin's aesthetic) to demonstrate how deep focus, which was one of the "natural" techniques of realism, can itself be manipulative through lighting effects and point of view.

11. The phatic function is composed of "messages serving to establish, to prolong, or to discontinue communication, to check whether the channel works..." (Roman Jakobson, "Linguistics and Poetics"). Bazin's sense of film is phatic in its understanding of film as a channel to something else; the best films are those that best maintain this channel, films that least call attention to themselves.

12. This is according to Eisenstein. As already noted in regard to Bazin, the single shot may well not be arbitrarily polysemous and, in fact, may already be coded *as an image*. One inadequacy of Eisenstein's theory is the extent to which he deemphasizes the single shot as a field of montage (and so, at some level, accepts Bazin's view of the single image as a window on the world). Much of this deemphasis is no doubt due to Eisenstein's personal need to leave behind his theatrical heritage—with its emphasis on mise-en-scène—as he moved on into the cinema.

   Eisenstein tends to read the film image as equivalent to the world in the image. This is the photographic tendency of the image which Eisenstein qualifies as anecdotal—things themselves are meaningful, are anecdotes of experience. Against this, Eisenstein calls for editing as a kind of de-anecdotalization (the term he uses in "Notes for a Film of *Kapital*").

   To be sure, Eisenstein did see the question of the frame, of meaning in the single image, as an issue: "Absolutely special will be the problem of the image and frame composition for *Kapital*. The ideology of the unequivocal frame must thoroughly be reconsidered. How, I can't yet tell" ("Notes for a Film," part 1, p. 24). But it was an issue that Eisenstein ultimately moved away from in his film research. Significantly, it is in other, more spatial arts, that Eisenstein most recognized the possibilities for a paradigmatic montage; at an early stage, he suggested that a new government building should have glass walls so that the actions in each office would juxtapose in a kind of synchronous montage.

13. *Non-indifferent nature* is the title of Eisenstein's most extended aesthetic inquiry into the dialectics of film (a two-volume French translation is available as *La non-indifférente nature*). The title is intended to suggest that nature, prefilmic actuality, is already dialectical and historical.

14. At different moments in his writing, Eisenstein valorizes conflict or a restful end to conflict. Aumont convincingly argues that this relates to Eisenstein's conception of history as the struggle toward the finality of socialism.

15. I should note that what Earle refers to as realism is more what I have referred to as actualism. Indeed, Earle's discussion, useful as it is for an examination of the problems of actualism, has no conception of a dialectical realism; in consequence, the only alternative he can suggest to the documentary realism he discusses is an "unrealism."

16. This attempt to find visual equivalents for concepts stayed with Eisenstein in his film work. At one point in his writings, for example, he suggests that images filmed upside down would be the best way to express the political concept of revolution ("Montage 1937").

17. On film as magical art, see Edgar Morin, *Le cinéma, ou l'homme imaginaire* (1956).

18. Despite the parallels often drawn between Eisenstein's work and Vgotsky's work on inner speech, what Vgotsky is dealing with seems much closer to a concept of inner monologue than of inner speech in the sense in which Eisenstein understands the concept. See Vygotsky, *Thought and Language* (1962), for a discussion of inner speech as private, internalized language.

19. For the script of these scenes, see the Appendix to Ivor Montagu, *With Eisenstein in Hollywood* (1969).

20. For *Marnie*, see "Hitchcock the Enunciator" (*Camera Obscura* 2, 1977); for *Psycho*, see "Psychosis, Neurosis, Perversion" (*Camera Obscura* 3/4, 1979).

21. On *Man With a Movie Camera* as a film investigating perception, and perception *as work*, see Stephen Crofts and Olivia Rose, "An Essay Towards *Man With a Movie Camera*" (*Screen*, 1977).

Chapter 3

1. For a further presentation of Jameson's view on the unitary, noncontradictory status of mass culture, see his "Reification and Utopia in Mass Culture," *Social Text* 1 (1979).

2. For the initial introduction of these concepts into film theory, see Christian Metz, "History/Discourse" in *Edinburgh 1976 Magazine*.

3. Indeed, Michel Foucault's suggestion in *Histoire de la sexualité: la volonté de savoir* (1976) that it is not in keeping quiet, but in openly confessing, that one most enters social relations, might serve as an interesting source of comparison for the exhibitionist status of film spectacle, which is itself a sort of confession; nowhere is this more true for the commercial film industry than in its recourse to the star as that figure who exhibits not only a self onscreen but who confesses his/her private life (or that version of the private life created by studio publicity) to allow spectators a kind of symbolic "hold" over the star.

4. The classic text of film criticism offering such an approach is the collective text by *Cahiers du Cinéma* on *Young Mr. Lincoln* (1970). This analysis, as with much of the analyses of structuring absences in bourgeois art, is heavily indebted to the theory of symptomatic reading proposed by Pierre Macherey in *Pour une théorie de la production littéraire* (1966).

5.   See, for example, the reading of *Grease* by the Manchester Society for Education in Film and Television reading group in *North by Northwest* 8 (1980).

6.   For a general theory of the avant-garde's adversarial stance, see Renato Poggioli, *The Theory of the Avant-Garde* (1971).

7.   Also of interest in this respect is Benjamin's essay "Surrealism," collected in *Reflections* (1978). Arguing that Marxism has to concern itself with the progressive as well as regressive elements of a movement like surrealism, Benjamin adopts a position similar to the Russian formalists. He suggests that surrealism's concern with processes of "illumination" was not a form of romantic escapism but a *profane* illumination, a process by which objects of everyday life are made strange: "to win the energies of intoxication for the revolution—this is the project about which Surrealism circles in all its books and enterprises" (p. 191). "Circles" implies both distance from and connection to, and Benjamin's goal is to emphasize the connection. Central to this task is the study of surrealism as an art of imagery, rather than metaphor—that is, an art which is always about something, even in its most distanced forms ("to organize pessimism [as did the surrealists] means nothing other than to expel moral *metaphor* from politics and to discover in political action a sphere reserved one hundred percent for images"—p. 191, my emphasis). In an almost throwaway line, Benjamin argues that "an action puts forth its own image" (p. 191); in my own analysis of the avant-garde in this chapter, my purpose will be to read, through metacommentary, some of the actions which put forth the images of the American avant-garde cinema.

8.   For an introduction to this aggressive moment in the avant-garde, see the discussion of "agonistic" and "antagonistic" avant-gardes in Poggioli, *The Theory of the Avant-Garde.*

9.   On the placement of the artist into the text of *Act of Seeing,* see Daniel H. Levoff's essay on the film in *Film Culture* 56-57 (1973).

10.   For an extended criticism of Sitney's approach, see Chuck Kleinhans, "Reading and Thinking about the Avant-Garde," *Jump Cut* 6 (1975).

11.   See Manfredo Tafuri, *Projet et utopie* (1979).

12.   Unfortunately, Jack Smith's *Flaming Creatures* (1964), which sounds like the paradigmatic film of this type, was unavailable for screening. For a suggestive essay on the film, see Susan Sontag, "Flaming Creatures," in *Against Interpretation* (1969).

13.   This sense of menace is present in earlier, non-American city symphonies such as Ruttman's *Berlin,* in which the physiology of the city includes an inevitable death.

14.   On the use of color in Ackerman, see Mary Jo Lakeland, "*The Color of Jeanne Dielman*" (*Camera Obscura* 3/4, 1979).

Chapter 4

1.   The reading that follows is not an attempt to claim the truth of Brecht, to read Brecht *à la lettre,* but to uncover *a* Brecht that has been repressed in dominant discourse on Brecht.

2.   For example, Colin MacCabe's influential essay "The Politics of Separation" (*Screen,* 1975/76) makes it seem as if Brecht were nothing but an investigator into the aesthetic effects of formal separation.

3.   At times, MacCabe's reading of Brecht approaches the novelistic. For example, on p. 103, MacCabe imagines an intersection of Brecht and Joyce in which there is a perfect meeting of the minds: "One can . . . indulge for a moment in fantasy—*Exiles* produced by Brecht while in Denmark in 1938, in exile and working on novels—that indeed might have been interesting."

4. See also the work of Janey Place on John Ford (in *Wide Angle,* 1978); Martin Walsh on Straub and Huillet (*Jump Cut* 4); and the general theoretical approach toward the deconstructive film in *Screen.*

5. On the ideological equivalence of philosophies of surface (the immediate coincidence of subject and object) and of depth (the eventual coincidence of subject and object), see the critique of empiricism, broadly defined, in Pierre Macherey, *Pour une théorie de la production littéraire* (1966).

6. See, for example, the final chapter of James Roy MacBean's *Film and Revolution* (1975) which calls for the dismantling of the Bazinian aesthetic as the first priority of a radical theory of film.

7. On the ways in which Bazin's approach turns out to be only one theory of film language among many, see Peter Wollen, "The Semiology of the Cinema," *Signs and Meaning in the Cinema* (1972).

8. Peter Wollen's analysis of *Citizen Kane* ("Semiotics and *Citizen Kane,*" *Film Reader,* 1975) is an important essay in this respect for the ways in which it polemically reads one of the films that is a cornerstone of the Bazinian approach in a way directly opposed to Bazin's reading of the film.

9. This, I would argue, is the case in several essays in *What is Cinema?* in which, unable to defend the Western on the grounds of realism, Bazin resorts to a number of alternate criteria: the Western's mythic force, for example.

10. For this argument, see (among others) Stephen Heath's influential "Narrative Space" (*Screen,* 1976).

11. Indeed, as Renato Poggioli points out (in *Theory of the Avant-Garde,* 1971, pp. 33-34.), even as politically conservative a critical movement as American New Criticism can be considered an avant-garde criticism in its emphasis on *contradiction* and *tension* as central components of artistic structure.

Chapter 5

1. For a summary of this and other Oshima films, see the appendix. I should note that all my comments are based on a screening of approximately half of Oshima's prodigious output. I have tried to view everything available in this country and in France.

2. For a representative critique of the film's supposed "theatricality," see Pascal Bonitzer, "Le cercle de la famille" (1980).

3. See, for example, the testimonies running through *Les femmes, la pornographie, l'érotisme* (ed. Hans and Lapouge, 1978) by women who have found in *Realm of the Senses* the triumph of an erotic, nonpornographic cinema. None of these testimonies refer to disjunctions in editing style.

4. For one general presentation of the post-structuralist valorization of the death-drive in conjunction with a general theory of textuality, see Jeffrey Mehlman, *Revolution and Repetition* (1977).

5. On the textualization of death in a fiction film like *Meet Me in St. Louis,* see Robin Wood, "The American Family Comedy: From *Meet Me in St. Louis* to *The Texas Chainsaw Massacre*" (*Wide Angle,* 1979).

6. An illuminating text in this respect is Oshima's "Banish Green" (available in French in Oshima, *Ecrits,* 1980). Oshima explains that he has consciously tried to banish the color green

in certain of his color films so as to avoid any suggestion of the natural world, of Rousseauistic or nostalgic solutions to the problems raised in the films.

7.   As, for example, on page 6: "We repeat a work of art as a singularity without a concept, and it is not by chance that a poem must be learned by heart. The head is the organ of exchanges, but the heart is the organ in love with repetition."

8.   I have not dealt with the work of Jean-Luc Godard here for several reasons. First, Godard as political artist has received excellent analysis elsewhere. But, more importantly, as Julia Lesage argues in her dissertation on Godard (1975), Godard's frequent use of a solitary hero who wanders through a chaotic world may still connect Godard to a romantic ideology rather than to a new conception of production and collective action. In *Tout Va Bien*, for example, self-reflexivity essentially drops out after the opening; nothing in the process of the film works to extend the voyage of political awareness on the part of the couple (Yves Montand, Jane Fonda) to the spectator in his/her political situation.

Bibliography

Abbott, Paul. "Authority." *Screen,* 20, n. 2 (Summer 1979), 11-64.

Aesthetics and Politics. Ed. Ronald Taylor. London: New Left Books, 1977.

Alter, Robert. *Partial Magic: The Novel as a Self-Conscious Genre.* Berkeley: University of California Press, 1975.

Althusser, Louis. *For Marx.* Trans. Ben Brewster. New York: Vintage Books, 1970.

_____. *Lenin and Philosophy and Other Essays.* Trans. Ben Brewster. New York: Monthly Review Press, 1971.

_____. *Réponse à John Lewis.* Paris: Francis Maspero, 1973.

Altman, Charles F. "Intratextual Rewriting: Textuality as Language Formation." *The Sign in Music and Literature.* Ed. Wendy Steiner. Austin: University of Texas Press, 1981.

Andrew, Dudley. *The Major Film Theories.* New York: Oxford University Press, 1976.

_____. *André Bazin.* New York: Oxford University Press, 1978.

Arnheim, Rudolf. *Film as Art.* 2d ed. Berkeley: University of California Press, 1957.

Aronowitz, Stanley. "Film—The Art Form of Late Capitalism." *Social Text,* 1 (Winter 1979), 110-129.

Auerbach, Erich. *Mimesis: The Representation of Reality in Western Literature.* Trans. Willard R. Trask. Princeton: Princeton University Press, 1953.

Augst, Bertrand. "The Order of [Cinematographic] Discourse." *Discourse,* 1 (Fall 1979), 39-57.

Aumont Jacques. *Montage Eisenstein.* Paris: Editions Albatros, 1979.

Barna, Yon. *Eisenstein.* Trans. Lise Hunter. Boston: Little, Brown and Co., 1973.

Barthes, Roland. *Writing Degree Zero and Elements of Semiology.* Trans. Annette Lavers and Colin Smith. Boston: Beacon Press, 1970.

_____. *S/Z.* Paris: Editions du Seuil. 1970.

_____. *L'Empire des signes.* Geneva: Editions d'Art Albert Skira, 1970.

_____. *Le Plaisir du texte.* Paris: Editions du Seuil, 1973.

_____. "En sortant du cinéma." *Communications,* 23 (1975), 104-07.

_____. *Image/Music/Text.* Ed. and trans. Stephen Heath. London: Fontana Books, 1977.

_____. *La chambre claire: Note sur la photographie.* Paris: Gallimard, 1980.

Baudrillard, Jean. *Pour une critique de l'économie politique du signe.* Paris: Gallimard, 1972.

_____. *The Mirror of Production.* Trans. and intro. Mark Poster. Milwaukee: Telos Press, 1975.

Baudry, Jean-Louis. "Ideological Effects of the Basic Cinematographic Apparatus." Trans. Alan Williams. *Film Quarterly,* 27, no. 2 (Winter 1974-75), 39-47.

_____. "The Apparatus." Trans. Bertrand Augst. *Camera Obscura,* 1 (Fall 1974), 104-126.

Bazin, André. *What is Cinema?* v. 1. Ed. and trans. Hugh Gray. Berkeley: University of California Press, 1967.

_____. *What is Cinema?* v. 2. Ed. and trans. Hugh Gray, Berkeley: University of California Press, 1971.

Bellour, Raymond. "The Obvious and the Code." Trans. Diane Matias. *Screen,* 15, n. 4 (Winter 1974-75), 7-17.

————. "The Unattainable Text." Trans. Diane Matias *Screen,* 16, no. 3 (Autumn 1975), 19-27.

————. "Hitchcock the Enunciator." Trans. Betrand Augst and Hilary Radner. *Camera Obscura,* 2 (Fall 1977), 66-91.

————. "Cine-Repetitions." Trans. Diane Matias. *Screen,* 20, n. 2 (Summer 1979), 65-72.

————. "Psychosis, Neurosis, Perversion." Trans. Nancy Huston. *Camera Obscura,* 3-4 (Winter 1979), 105-132.

Benjamin, Walter. *Charles Baudelaire: A Lyric Poet in the Era of High Capitalism.* Trans. Harry Zohn. London: New Left Books, 1973.

————. *Understanding Brecht.* Trans. Anna Bostock. London: New Left Books, 1973.

————. *Illuminations.* Trans. Harry Zohn. Ed. Hannah Arendt. New York: Schocken Books, 1969.

————. *Reflections.* Trans. Edmund Jephcott. Ed. Peter Demetz. New York: Harcourt, Brace, Jovanovich, 1978.

Bennett, Tony. *Formalism and Marxism.* London: Methuen and Co., Ltd., 1979.

Berger, John. *Ways of Seeing.* New York: Penguin Books, 1977.

Bergstrom, Janet. "Enunciation and Sexual Difference." *Camera Obscura,* 3-4 (Winter 1979), 33-69.

————. "Alternation, Segmentation, Hypnosis: an Interview with Raymond Bellour." *Camera Obscura,* 3-4 (Winter 1979), 71-103.

Bonitzer, Pascal. "Le cercle de famille." *Cahiers du Cinéma,* 309 (March 1980), 5-8.

Bordwell, David. "Eisenstein's Epistemological Shift." *Screen,* 15, n. 4 (Winter 1974-75), 29-46.

Branigan, Edward. "Subjectivity under Siege—from Fellini's *8 1/2* to Oshima's *The Man Who Left His Will on Film,*" *Screen,* 19, n. 1 (Spring 1978), 7-40.

Brecht, Bertolt. *Brecht on Theatre.* Ed. and trans. John Willett. New York: Hill and Wang, 1964.

————. *Sur le réalisme.* Trans. Andre Gisselbrecht. Paris: L'Arche, 1970.

————. *Sur le cinéma.* Trans. Jean-Louis Lefebvre and Jean-Pierre Lefebvre. Paris: L'Arche, 1970.

————. *Les arts et la révolution.* Trans. Bernard Lortholary. Paris: L'Arche, 1970.

Brenkman, John. "Mass Media: From Collective Experience to the Culture of Privatisation." *Social Text,* 1 (Winter 1979), 94-109.

————. "Deconstruction and the Social Text." *Social Text,* 1 (Winter 1979), 186-188.

Brewster, Ben. "The Fundamental Reproach (Brecht)." *Cine-Tracts,* 3 (Spring-Summer 1977), 44-53.

Britton, Andrew. "Sexuality and Power (part 1)." *Framework,* 6 (Autumn 1977), 7-11.

————. "Sexuality and Power (part 2)." *Framework,* 7-8 (Spring 1978), 4-11.

Brown, Robert K. "Interview with Bruce Conner." *Film Culture,* 33, 15-16.

Bucci-Glucksmann, Christine. "Deconstruction et Critique Marxiste de la Philosophie." *L'Arc,* 54, 20-32.

Burch, Noel. *A Theory of Film Practice.* Trans. Helen Lane. Preface by Annette Michelson. New York: Praeger Publishers, 1973.

————. "Avant-Garde or Vanguard." *Afterimage,* 6 (Summer 1976), 52-63.

————. "Porter, or ambivalence." *Screen,* 19, n. 4 (Winter 1978-79), 91-105.

————. *To the Distant Observer: Form and Meaning in the Japanese Film.* Berkeley: University of California Press, 1979.

Burch, Noel and Dana, Jorge. "Positions." *Afterimage,* 5 (Spring 1974), 40-65.

Carroll, Noel. "Avant-Garde Film and Film Theory." Paper presented at Society for Cinema Studies Annual Conference (March 1979).

Cohen, Keith. *Film and Fiction: The Dynamics of Exchange.* New Haven: Yale University Press, 1979.

Comolli, Jean-Louis and Narboni, Jean. "Cinema/Ideology/Criticism." *Movies and Methods.* Ed. Bill Nichols. Berkeley: University of California Press, 1976.

Comolli, Jean-Louis. "Idéologie et Technique." *Cahiers du Cinéma,* 229 (May-June 1971), 10-24.

Conner, Bruce. "Bruce Conner." *Film Comment*, 5, n. 4 (Winter 1969), 18-20.

Cook, Pam. "Teaching Avant-Garde Film." *Screen Education*, 32-33 (Autumn-Winter 1979-80), 83-97.

Coward, Rosalind and Ellis, John. *Language and Materialism: Developments in Semiology and the Theory of the Subject*. London: Routledge and Kegan Paul, 1977.

Crofts, and Stephen and Rose, Oliva. "An Essay Towards *Man with a Movie Camera*." *Screen*, 18, n. 1 (Spring 1977), 9-58.

Culler, Jonathan. *Structuralist Poetics: Structuralism, Linguistics, and the Study of Literature*. Ithaca: Cornell University Press, 1975.

———. "Semiology and Deconstruction." *Poetics Today*, 1, n. 1-2 (Autumn 1972), 137-141.

Curtis, David. *Experimental Cinema*. New York: Universe Books, 1971.

Debord, Guy. *La société du spectacle*. Paris: Editions Champ libre, 1971.

Deleuze, Gilles. *Différence et répétition*. Paris: PUF, 1968.

De Man, Paul. *Blindness and Insight: Essays in the Rhetoric of Contemporary Criticism*. New York: Oxford University Press, 1971.

Derrida, Jacques. *L'écriture et la différence*. Paris: Editions du Seuil, 1967.

———. *De la grammatologie*. Paris: Editions de Minuit, 1967.

———. "Structure, Sign, and Play in the Discourse of the Human Sciences." *The Structuralist Controversy: The Languages of Criticism and the Sciences of Man*. Ed. and trans. Richard Macksey and Eugenio Donato. Baltimore: Johns Hopkins University Press, 1971.

———. "Freud and the Scene of Writing." Trans. Jeffrey Mehlman. *Yale French Studies*, 33 (1972) 104-140.

Discourse. "The Cinematic Apparatus as Social Institution—An Interview with Christian Metz." N. 1 (Fall 1979), 7-37.

Dyer, Richard. *Light Entertainment*. London: British Film Institute, 1973.

———. *Stars*. London: British Film Institute, 1979.

Eagleton, Terry. *Criticism and Ideology*. London: New Left Books, 1976.

———. "Ideology, Fiction, Narrative." *Social Text*, 2 (Summer 1979), 62-80.

Earle, William. "The Revolt Against Realism in Film." *Film Theory and Criticism*. Ed. Gerald Mast and Marshall Cohen. New York: Oxford University Press, 1974.

Eco, Umberto. *A Theory of Semiotics*. Bloomington: Indiana University Press, 1976.

———. "Articulations of the Cinematic Code." *Movies and Methods*. Ed. Bill Nichols. Berkeley: University of California Press, 1976.

Ehrenreich, Barbara. "*Mary Hartman*: A World Out of Control." *Socialist Revolution*, 30 (October-December 1976), 133-137.

Eikhenbaum, Boris. "Problems of Film Stylistics." Trans. Thomas Aman. *Screen*, 15, no. 3 (Autumn, 1974), 7-32.

Eisenstein, Sergei. *The Film Sense*. Ed. and trans. Jay Leyda. New York: Harcourt Brace and World, 1947.

———. *Film Form*. Ed. and trans. Jay Leyda. New York: Harcourt Brace and World, 1949.

———. "Sur la question d'une approche materialiste de la forme." *Cahiers du Cinéma*, 220-221 (1968), 8-17.

———. "Structure, Montage, Passage." *Le Montage*. Paris: Editions du Seuil, 1968.

———. "Montage of Attractions." *The Drama Review*, 18, n. 1, 77-84.

———. "The Gothic." Trans. Roberta Reeder. *Oppositions*, n. 11, 111-115.

———. "Notes for a Film of *Kapital* (part 1)." *October*, 2 (Summer 1976), 3-26.

———. "Notes for a Film of *Kapital* (part 2)." *October*, 3 (Spring 1977), 70-81.

———. *La non-indifférente nature* (2 volumes). Trans. Luda and Jean Schnitzer. Paris: October 18, 1978.

———. *Esquisses et dessins*. Ed. Jacques Aumont, Bernard Eisenschitz, and Jean Narboni. Paris: Editions de l'Etoile, 1978.

Eizykman, Claudine. *La jouissance-cinéma*. Paris: Union Generale d'Editions, 1976.

Ellis, John. "Made in Ealing." *Screen,* 16, n. 1 (Spring 1975), 78-127.

Enzensberger, Hans Magnus. *The Consciousness Industry: On Literature, Politics, and the Media.* New York: Seabury Press, 1974.

Ewen, Stuart. *Captains of Consciousness: Advertising and the Social Roots of Consumer Culture.* New York: McGraw-Hill, 1977.

Farber, Manny. *Negative Space.* New York: Praeger Publishing, 1971.

Feldman, Seth. *Evolution of Style in the Early Work of Dziga Vertov.* New York: Arno Press, 1977.

Foucault, Michel. *La volonté de savoir: histoire de la sexualité 1.* Paris: Gallimard, 1976.

Freud, Sigmund. *Beyond the Pleasure Principle.* New York: W.W. Norton and Co., 1961.

――――. *Introduction to Psychoanalysis.* New York: Pocket Books, 1975.

Gidal, Peter, ed. *Structural Film Anthology.* London: British Film Institute, 1978.

――――. "The Anti-Narrative." *Screen,* 20, n. 2 (Summer 1979), 73-92.

Godard, Jean-Luc and Gorin, Jean-Pierre. "Transcript of *Letter to Jane.*" *Cinemonkey* (Fall 1978), 11-19.

Goldmann, Lucien. *Pour une sociologie du roman.* Paris: Gallimard, 1964.

Gombrich, Ernst. *Art and Illusion: A Study in the Psychology of Pictorial Representation.* Princeton: Princeton University Press, 1960 (rev. 1972).

Guerard, Albert J. *The Triumph of the Novel: Dickens, Dostoyevsky, Faulkner.* New York: Oxford University Press, 1976.

Hadjinicolaou, Nicos. "Sur l'idéologie de l'avant-gardisme." *Histoire et critique des arts,* 6 (July 1978), 49-76.

Hans, M.-F. and Lapouge, G. *Les femmes, la pornographie, l'érotisme.* Paris: Editions du Seuil, 1978.

Heath, Stephen. *Vertige du deplacement: lecture de Barthes.* Paris: Fayard, 1974.

――――. "Narrative Space." *Screen,* 17, n. 3 (Autumn 1976), 68-112.

――――. "Anata Mo." *Screen,* 17, n. 4 (Winter 1976-77), 49-66.

――――. "*Jaws,* Ideology, and Film Theory." *Film Reader,* 2 (January 1977), 166-168.

――――. "The Question Oshima." *Ophuls.* Ed. Paul Willemen. London: British Film Institute, 1978.

――――. "Difference." *Screen,* 19, n. 3 (Autumn 1978), 51-112.

――――. "Afterword to Gidal's 'The Anti-Narrative.'" *Screen,* 20, n. 2 (Summer 1979), 93-99.

――――. "The Turn of the Subject." *Cine-Tracts,* 7-8 (Summer-Fall 1979), 32-48.

Heath, Stephen and Skirrow, Gillian. "Television: A World in Action." *Screen,* 18, n. 2 (Summer 1977), 7-59.

Henderson, Brian. *A Critique of Film Theory.* New York: E.P. Dutton and Co., 1980.

Henry, Michel. "Entretien avec Nagisa Oshima." *Positif,* 206 (May 1978), 7-10.

Hindess, Barry and Hirst, P.Q. *Pre-Capitalist Modes of Production.* London: Routledge and Kegan Paul, 1975.

Jakobson, Roman. "On Realism in Art." *Readings in Russian Poetics: Formalist and Structuralist Views.* Ed. and trans. Ladislav Matejka and Krystyna Pomorska. Cambridge: The M.I.T. Press, 1971.

――――. "Linguistics and Poetics." *The Structuralists from Marx to Levi-Strauss.* Ed. Richard and Fernande DeGeorge. New York: Anchor Books, 1972.

Jameson, Fredric. "Metacommentary." *PMLA,* 86, n. 1 (January 1971), 9-18.

――――. *Marxism and Form: Twentieth Century Dialectical Theories of Literature.* Princeton: Princeton University Press, 1971.

――――. *The Prison-House of Language: A Critical Account of Structuralism and Russian Formalism.* Princeton: Princeton University Press, 1972.

――――. "Criticism in History." *Weapons of Criticism: Marxism in America and the Literary Tradition.* Ed. Norman Rudich. Palo Alto: Ramparts Press, 1976.

――――. "Reification and Utopia in Mass Culture." *Social Text,* 1 (1979), 130-148.

_____. *Fables of Aggression: Wyndham Lewis, The Modernist as Fascist.* Berkeley: University of California Press, 1979.

Johnston, Claire, ed. *History/Production/Memory. Edinburgh 1977 Magazine,* 1977.

Kermode, Frank. *The Sense of An Ending: Studies in the Theory of Fiction.* New York: Oxford University Press, 1967.

_____. "Novels: Recognition and Deception." *Critical Inquiry,* 1, n. 1 (September 1974), 103-121.

Kleinhans, Chuck. "Reading and Thinking about the Avant-Garde." *Jump Cut,* 6 (March-April 1973), 21-25.

_____. "Swinging on Burch's Theory." *Jump Cut,* 10-11 (Summer 1976), 64-66.

Kofman, Sarah. *Camera Obscura de l'idéologie.* Paris: Editions Galilee, 1973.

Kristeva, Julia. *Semiotike: recherches pour une semanalyse.* Paris: Editions du Seuil, 1969.

_____. *La révolution du langage poétique.* Paris: Editions du Seuil, 1974.

_____. "Signifying Practices and Modes of Production." Trans. Geoffrey Nowell-Smith. *Edinburgh 1976 Magazine* (1976), 40-52.

_____. "Modern Theatre Does Not Take (A) Place." *Sub-Stance,* 18-19 (1977), 131-134.

Kuntzel, Thierry. "Savoir, Pouvoir, Voir (Allégorie d'une Caverne)." *CA Cinéma,* 2, n. 7-8 (May 1975), 85-97.

de Kuyper, Eric. "Le mauvais genre." *CA Cinéma,* 18 (1980), 44-49.

Lakeland, Mary Jo. "The Color of *Jeanne Dielman.*" *Camera Obscura,* 3-4 (1979), 216-218.

Lapsley, Rob. "Economies of Desire." *North by Northwest,* 8 (Autumn 1979), 6-11.

Lecourt, Dominique. *Marxism and Epistemology: Bachelard, Canghuilhem, and Foucault.* Trans. Ben Brewster. London: New Left Books, 1975.

LeGrice, Malcolm. "Talk delivered at the London Film Co-op, February 10, 1976." *Unpublished manuscript.*

_____. *Abstract Film and Beyond.* Cambridge: The M.I.T. Press, 1977.

Lehman, Peter. "Style, Function, and Ideology: A Problem in Film History." *Film Reader,* 4 (1979), 72-80.

Lesage, Julia. *The Films of Jean-Luc Godard and Their Use of Brechtian Dramatic Theory.* Unpublished Ph.D. dissertation. Indiana University, 1975.

Levitin, Jacqueline. *Jean-Luc Godard: Aesthetics as Revolution.* Unpublished Ph.D. dissertation. Indiana University, 1975.

Levi-Strauss, Claude. "The Structural Analysis of Myth." *The Structuralists from Marx to Levi-Strauss.* Ed. Richard and Fernande DeGeorge. New York: Anchor Books, 1972.

Levoff, Daniel, H. "Brakhage's *The Act of Seeing With One's Own Eyes.*" *Film Culture,* 56-57 (Spring 1973), 73-80.

Leyda, Jay. *Kino: a History of the Russian and Soviet Film.* New York: Collier Books, 1973.

Lotman, Jurij. *Semiotics of the Cinema.* Trans. Mark E. Suino. Ann Arbor, Michigan: Slavic Contributions, 1976.

Lukács, Georg. *Realism in Our Time: Literature and the Class Struggle.* Trans. John and Necke Mander. New York: Harper and Row Publishers, 1971.

_____. *Writer and Critic and Other Essays.* Ed. and trans. Arthur D. Kath. New York: Grosset and Dunlap, 1974.

Lyotard, Jean-François. "Acinema." Trans. Paisley Livingston. *Wide Angle,* 2, n. 3 (1978), 52-59.

_____. "One of the Things at Stake in the Woman's Struggle." *Sub-Stance,* 20 (1978), 9-17.

_____. *La condition post-moderne.* Paris: Les Editions de Minuit, 1979.

MacBean, James. *Film and Revolution.* Bloomington: Indiana University Press, 1975.

MacCabe, Colin. "The Politics of Separation." *Screen,* 10, n. 4 (Winter 1975-76), 46-61.

_____. "Theory and Film: Principles of Realism and Pleasure." *Screen,* 17, n. 3 (Autumn 1976), 7-26.

_____. *James Joyce and the Revolution of the Word.* London: The MacMillan Press, 1978.

Macherey, Pierre. *Pour une théorie de la production littéraire.* Paris: Maspero, 1966.

———. "The Problem of Reflection." *Sub-Stance*, 15 (1976), 6-20.

Manchester Society for Education in Film and Television Reading Group. *"Grease." North by Northwest*, 8 (Autumn 1979), 24.

Marcuse, Herbert. *Eros and Civilisation: A Philosophical Inquiry into Freud.* New York: Vintage Book, 1962.

———. *The Aesthetic Dimension.* Boston: Beacon Press Books, 1978.

Marx, Karl and Engels, Fredrich. *The German Ideology.* New York: International Publishers, 1970.

Mast, Gerald. *Film/Cinema/Movie: A Theory of Experience.* New York: Harper and Row Publishers, 1977.

Mattelart, Armand. "The Nature of Communications Practices in a Dependent Society." Trans. Dana B. Polan. *Latin American Perspectives,* 5, n. 1 (Winter 1978), 13-34.

Mayne, Judith. *The Ideologies of Metacinema.* Unpublished Ph.D. dissertation. SUNY at Buffalo, 1975.

Mehlman, Jeffrey. *Revolution and Repetition.* Berkeley: University of California Press, 1977.

Mellen, Joan. "Nagisa Oshima." *Voices from the Japanese Cinema.* New York: Liveright, 1975.

Metz, Christian. *Essais sur la signification au cinéma.* (2 v.) Paris: Editions Klincksieck, 1975.

———. *Langage et cinéma.* Paris: Librairie Larousse, 1971.

Michaels, Walter, Benn. "Against Formalism: The Autonomous Text in Legal and Literary Interpretation" *Poetics Today,* 1, n. 1-2 (Autumn 1979), 23-34.

Michelson, Annette. "The Politics of Illusionism." *Artforum,* 6, n. 10 (1968), 66-71.

———. Preface to Noel Burch, *Theory of Film Practice.* New York: Praeger Books, 1973.

———. "Reading Eisenstein Reading *Capital* (part 1)." *October,* 2 (Summer 1976), 27-38.

———. "Reading Eisenstein Reading *Capital* (part 2)." *October,* 3 (Spring 1977), 82-89.

Modleski, Tania. *Loving with a Vengeance: Mass-Produced Fantasies for Women.* Hamden, CT.: Archon Books, 1982.

Montagu, Ivor. *With Eisenstein in Hollywood.* New York: International Publishers, 1969.

Morin, Edgar. *Le cinéma ou l'homme imaginaire.* Paris: Les Editions de Minuit, 1956.

———. *Les stars.* Paris: Les editions de Minuit, 1957.

Morris, Charles. *Foundations of the Theory of Signs.* Chicago: University of Chicago Press, 1938.

Moussinac, Leon. *Sergei Eisenstein.* Paris: Editions Seghers, 1964.

Mulvey, Laura. "Visual Pleasure and Narrative Cinema." *Screen,* 16, n. 3 (Autumn, 1975), 6-18.

Noiret, Hubert. "Entretien avec Nagisa Oshima." *Positif,* 181 (May 1976), 49-53.

Nowell-Smith, Geoffrey. "A Note on History/Discourse." *Edinburgh 1976 Magazine,* 1976, 26-31.

Oshima, Nagisa. *Ecrits (1956-1978): Dissolution et jaillissement.* Trans. Jean-Paul le Pape. Paris: Gallimard, 1980.

———. "Plaidoyer: le drapeau de l'éros flotte dans les cieux." Trans. Jean-Paul le Pape. *Cahiers du Cinéma,* 309 (March 1980), 9-12.

Pecheux, Michel. *Les vérités de la Palice: linguistique, semantique, philosophie.* Paris: Maspero, 1975.

Penley, Constance. "The Avant-Garde and Its Imaginary." *Camera Obscura,* 2 (Fall 1977), 3-33.

Place, Janey. "*Young Mr. Lincoln,* 1939." *Wide Angle,* 2, n. 4 (1978), 28-35.

Pleynet, Marcelin. "The 'Left' Front of Art." Trans. Susan Bennett. *Screen Reader.* London: Society for Education in Film and Television, 1977. 225-243.

Poggioli, Renato. *The Theory of Avant-Garde.* Trans. Gerald Fitzgerald. New York: Harper and Row, 1971.

Polan, Dana, B. "Review of *Film/Cinema/Movie.*" *Journal of Aesthetics and Art Criticism,* 38, n. 3 (Spring, 1979), 386-387.

Ropars, Marie-Claire. *See* Sorlin, Pierre.

Rose, Jacqueline. "Paranoia and the Film System." *Screen,* 17, n.4 (Winter 1976-77), 49-66.

Rosen, Philip. "Difference and Displacement in *Seventh Heaven.*" *Screen,* 18, n.2 (Summer 1977), 89-104.

Rosenthal, Michael. "Ideology, Determinism, and Relative Autonomy." *Jump Cut*, 17 (Spring 1978), 19-22.

Russell, Lee. "Sam Fuller." *New Left Review*, 23 (January-February 1964), 86-89.

Sartre, Jean-Paul. *Critique de la raison dialectique*. Paris: Gallimard, 1960.

Screen Reader 1. London: Society for Education in Film and Television, 1977.

Shklovsky, Viktor. "Poetry and Prose in Cinematography." Trans. T.L. Aman. *Russian Formalism*, Ed. S. Bann and J.E. Bowlit. New York: Harper and Row, 1973.

Simon, Jean-Paul. *Le filmique et la comique: essai sur le film comique*. Paris: Editions Albatros, 1979.

———. "La production du texte filmique: structures, structuration, histoire." *Ca Cinema*, 18 (1980), 50-65.

Singer, Marilyn, ed. *A History of American Avant-Garde Cinema*. New York: American Federation for the Arts, 1976.

Sitney, P. Adam. *Visionary Cinema: The American Avant-Garde*. New York: Oxford University Press, 1974.

Sontag, Susan. "Jack Smith's *Flaming Creatures*." *Against Interpretation*. New York: Dell Publishing, 1969.

Sorlin, Pierre and Ropars, Marie-Claire. *Octobre: Ecriture et Idéologie*. Paris: Editions Albatros, 1976.

Spitzer, Leo. "American Advertising Explained as Popular Art." *Essays on English and American Literature*. Princeton: Princeton University Press, 1962.

Steiner, George. *On Difficulty and Other Essays*. London: Oxford University Press, 1978.

Swallow, Norman. *Eisenstein: A Documentary Portrait*. London: George Allen and Unwin, Ltd., 1976.

Tafuri, Manfredo. *Projet et utopie: de l'avant-garde à la metropole*. Trans. Françoise Brun. Paris: Dunod, 1979.

Thompson, E.P. *The Poverty of Theory and other Essays*. London: Merlin Press, 1978.

Thompson, Kristin. "*Ivan the Terrible* and Stalinist Russia: A Reexamination." *Cinema Journal*, 17, n. 1 (Fall 1977), 30-43.

———. "The Duplicitous Text: An Analysis of *Stage Fright*." *Film Reader*, 2 (January 1977), 52-64.

———. "The Concept of Cinematic Excess." *Cine-Tracts*, 2 (Spring-Summer 1977), 54-63.

Thompson, Rick. "*Duck Amuck*." *Film Comment*, 11, n. 1 (January-February 1975), 39-43.

Tudor, Andrew. *Theories of Film*. New York: The Viking Press, 1973.

Vertov, Dziga. *Articles, journaux, projets*. Paris: 10/18, 1972.

Vgotsky, Lev. *Thought and Language*. Trans. Eugenia Hanfmann and Gertrude Vakar. Cambridge: The M.I.T. Press, 1962.

Voloshinov, V.N. *Marxism and the Philosophy of Language*. Trans. Ladislaw Matejka and I.R. Titunik. New York: Seminar Press, 1973.

Walsh, Martin. "Political Formations in the Cinema of Jean-Marie Straub." *Jump Cut*, 4 (November-December 1974), 12-18.

———. "Noel Burch's Film Theory." *Jump Cut*, 10-11 (Summer 1976), 61-63.

Watt, Ian. *The Rise of the Novel: Studies in Defoe, Richardson and Fielding*. Berkeley: University of California Press, 1957.

White, Hayden. *Metahistory: The Historical Imagination in Nineteenth Century Europe*. Baltimore: The Johns Hopkins University Press, 1973.

Williams, Raymond. *Keywords: A Vocabulary of Culture and Society*. New York: Oxford University Press, 1976.

———. *Marxism and Literature*. New York, Oxford University Press, 1977.

———. "A Lecture on Realism." *Screen*, 18, n. 1 (Spring 1977), 61-74.

Wollen, Peter. *Signs and Meaning in the Cinema*. Bloomington: Indiana University Press, 1969 (rev. 1972).

_____. "Semiotics and *Citizen Kane*." *Film Reader*, 1 (1975), 9-15.

_____. "Ontology and Materialism in Film." *Screen*, 17, n.1 (Spring 1976), 7-23.

_____. "Photography and Aesthetics." *Screen*, 19, n. 4 (Winter 1978-79), 9-28.

Wood, Michael. *America in the Movies, or Santa Maria, It Had Slipped My Mind*. New York: Basic Books, 1975.

Wood, Robin. "The American Family Comedy from *Meet Me in St. Louis* to *Texas Chainsaw Massacre*." *Wide Angle*, 3, n.2 (1979), 5-11.

Zimmer, Christian. *Procès du spectacle*. Paris: PUF, 1977.

Index